Ethics and the Full-Breasted Richness of Life

Richard P. Mullin

AllrOneofUs Publishing
Baltimore, Md & Huntsville, Al

ETHICS AND THE FULL-BREASTED RICHNESS OF LIFE

First edition. September 4, 2020.

Updated edition. April 4, 2022

Copyright © 2019 Richard P. Mullin.

ISBN: 978-1393011507

Written by Richard P. Mullin.

Table of Contents

To Marian.

I also thank the many members of the Society for the Advancement of American philosophy whose writings and conversations have helped me immensely. I will name some at the risk of over-looking others who benefitted me. Randall Auxier, Michael Broderick, Judith Green, Jacquelyn Kegley, Mary Mahowald, Kelly Parker, and Frank Oppenheim, S.J.

Thanks too, to Mike Susko who made me aware of Draft2digital, and to all the students in my classes over the years, from whom I probably learned at least as much as I taught.

FOREWORD

Many years ago, I was a student of Rich Mullin who taught me a range of philosophy from the ancient Greeks to the modern day. He had the gift of clearly presenting complex ideas. The clarity became even more apparent in his teaching of American philosophy, a national treasure which is largely untapped. I witness that for myself, as I drew upon these principles which served as useful touchstones for my life. In culminating his work of teaching for decades, Rich offers this profound wisdom to you in an accessible way.

This is a book that keeps drawing you in with successive gems of wisdom, which can usefully inform and guide our thinking and actions. A guiding principle is that to recognize the importance of *loyalty* to causes and the recognition of the value of diverse causes which other people hold. Together, this works to bring about the greatest good for our community and the world.

The combination of philosophic wisdom and psychological depth is rare. This work would serve as an ideal companion book for an ethics class, one which would give students guidance for living in tune with a moral compass. The end result of paying attention to ethics is that we are enabled to live a richer and fuller life.

Michael A. Susko M.S.

INTRODUCTION

The title of this work derives from a letter that Charles Sanders Pierce wrote to Josiah Royce on June 30, 1913. Pierce said he regretted that while his own logic provided a lot of security, meaning avoidance of error, it lacked what he called uberty, from the Latin *ubertas*, meaning fecundity and nourishment that a mother provides for her offspring. Royce resolved to apply the notion of uberty to his own leading ideas: freedom, duty, and goodness. Royce's ethics not only teach us to avoid doing wrong but enable us to promote the good of harmony over the evil of chaotic disharmony. The original title of this book reflects this: *Beyond Right and Wrong: Ethics and Nourishing the Good.*

Royce lived and worked more than a century ago. However, ethics books often tap into bygone philosophers such as Aristotle (384-322 BC), Immanuel Kant (1724-1804), and John Stuart Mill (1806-1873). My contention is that Royce's ideas not only speak to us in a timely way, but that they involve insights that have been neglected and that could enrich all of our conversations and practices that involve living a better and more full life.

CHAPTER 1
Leading Principles of Ethics

Common Approaches to Ethics

Writers generally define ethics as the systematic study of right and wrong human actions. This definition captures much of what constitutes ethics, but a complete definition must go further. *Ethics should also study and develop ways to promote and nourish the good.* An objection often heard throughout any ethics course takes the form of the question, "Who is to say what is good?" Students may ask the question seriously or cynically, but the short answer is that everyone must have his or her say. The longer answer, which is the theme of this work, and of any good ethics course, argues that you and I can improve our ability to understand the good and to see more clearly that some things are objectively better than others. Everyone has the right to an opinion, but some opinions are better, meaning truer than others.

Is this position defensible? Are some things objectively better than others? This issue will be taken up after a few more remarks about the way ethics is often taught.

Ethics books and courses often present arguments for opposing sides of controversial issues and invite the students or readers to debate the two sides. Another common approach offers a menu of theories and asks the reader to speculate on how advocates of each theory would deal with the issues. While these methods may be useful in expanding the reader's knowledge of the complexity of issues, such knowledge is not sufficient for a true insight into ethics. Looking over a variety of theories and ethical positions without some criterion for evaluating them might lead to relativism and even skepticism, the belief that nothing is true or false in ethics. The whole enterprise of ethics may appear to be an exercise in rhetoric similar to a debate topic in which a team argues the affirmative position in the morning and the negative in the afternoon. Some will say, "Like it or not, that's the way it is—there are no objective truths in ethics."

Understanding the Good as Teleological Harmony

In the following pages, I will attempt to show that the *good* is real and not merely "in the eye of the beholder," and that our task as human beings is to nourish the *good*. Near the end of his life, American philosopher, Charles Sanders Peirce, founder of pragmatism, semiotics, and much of modern logic, wrote to his friend Josiah Royce and lamented that his own logic emphasized security but was lacking in *uberty*. By security he meant that it provided a method of avoiding error. He invented the word "uberty" from the Latin word *ubertas,* which he translated as "the full-breasted richness of life." He meant that logic should be fertile and nourishing, as a mother is to a child.[1] Royce agreed, and the following pages will show that Royce worked at applying the notion of nourishment to his three ethical categories: autonomy, duty, and the *good.*[2]

The paradox of autonomy and duty is balanced by the cardinal virtue of loyalty, which serves as a foundation of all virtue.[3] Royce developed a notion of the *good* that is rich in psychological and metaphysical insight. His idea of the *good* cannot be understood apart from the developmental process by which we come to know the good. For the present we can jump ahead to a description of *good* as harmony that overcomes evil disharmony.[4] The *good* not only brings together the conflicts that we experience between autonomy and duty, but constitutes the ethical purpose of our personal life-plan and our social interactions. Since the *good,* as harmony constitutes our purpose, we may call it "teleological harmony," a term that will be used throughout this book. Human beings have the duty to work toward the greatest possible harmony, or integration, as free autonomous individuals.

Following this insight, the task of an ethics book must go beyond helping the reader avoid moral error. Ethics must also, and more importantly, clarify the meaning of *good* and develop ways to promote the *good*. The ethical insights of Josiah Royce can take us a long way to achieving this goal.

The purpose of this book consists neither in giving a historical account of how Royce dealt with the problems of his time, nor in trying to guess what he "would say" about a particular contemporary situation. The point, rather, is to find better ways to approach the issues of our time, enriched and enlivened by Royce's insights. Like the pragmatists, William James and Charles S. Peirce, with whom Royce was closely associated, Royce maintained that ideas are purposeful and serve as tools for handling the issues that confront us. And, like James and Peirce, Royce followed the pragmatic axiom that thoughts are meaningful only if they are purposeful as plans of action. The philosophical insights called on in this book are not limited to those of Royce. Ancient and contemporary thinkers are also cited, but the guiding principles will be those of Royce. His ethical insights, as I will attempt to show, provide an eminently clear and attractive idea of the *good,* along with an admirably integrated approach to the individual flourishing and to communal responsibility.

Distinguishing True from False Opinions

An obstacle to a rational conversation on ethical issues is expressed by the often-asked questions: "Can we call opinions either true or false?[5] Aren't they just opinions?" When we want to dismiss a statement that we disagree with, we often say, "That's your opinion." This legitimate objection calls for a brief review and preview of the meaning of truth and falsity. I call this a review because the reader has certainly considered the meaning of true and false statements in other areas of life. I call it a preview because in the context of this book, the notion of true and false statements must be applied to issues of right and wrong, good and bad. The study of ethics invites the learners to think about ideas at every step and to consider whether they can accept them as true. To agree or disagree and to give reasons for a position signifies intellectual development and promotes further development. To reject ethical opinions without consideration is a sign of intellectual and moral flabbiness.

In affirming that some opinions are better than others or that some are true and others false, I do not presuppose that my opinions are necessarily the best or most true. We can each improve our view of reality only by making a lifelong process of learning and refining our opinions. As a first step, we need to clarify what we mean by opinions. Opinions consist of beliefs that we express as statements. Statements and beliefs hold true or false. When we express an opinion, we do not have absolute certainty that our opinion holds true, but we *think* that it does. We assume that if we knew everything that involves the particular issue, we would know that our opinion is true. But in fact, we do not know everything that we need to know, and so our opinion remains uncertain. To take an example not directly involving ethics, suppose the owners of a business think it would be a good idea to borrow money to expand their facilities. In their opinion, the expansion will increase their profits, enable them to hire more people, and improve their own lives and that of their community. The owners are implying that if they knew all the factors that would affect their business, they would know that good business sense calls for expansion at this time. In fact, they do not know all the factors, so their opinion might prove wrong leading to bankruptcy, harming themselves and others.

In most important areas of our lives, we must act without absolute certainty. We are more likely to form true opinions when we have a rich understanding of the area with which we are dealing. For example, a medical opinion from an examining physician carries weight that the mere opinion of an uninformed person does not. And yet, the patient may want to get a "second opinion." Therefore, developing our knowledge in areas in which we make ethical decisions holds a high priority. Much ethical misconduct results from tunnel vision and moral myopia.[6] We each have a pressing ethical duty to pay attention to the wide view so that we know who is affected by our decisions, <u>and</u> the long view, so that we see as far as possible what the long-term effect of our action will be. The American philosopher, John Dewey, suggested that the moral virtues ought to include "wide sympathy, keen sensitiveness, persistence in the face of the disagreeable, and balance of interests enabling us to undertake the work of analysis and decision intelligently."[7] These qualities help us make good decisions in ethics and in every other aspect of life.

Distinguishing Good from Bad Possibilities

The study of ethics must emphasize potential. Ethical questions do not reside in fully complete individuals pondering unchanging present situations. *Rather, ethics opens windows to what our world and our conscious selves can become.* The discussion of realizing potential implies that some potentials are better than others. We all have the potential to become productive, creative, loving members of our communities. But we also have the potential to become criminals, freeloaders, or mean-spirited people who make life miserable for everyone we encounter. We have the potential to become worse instead of better. Like a hammer, we have the potential to build or to break things. To know the difference, we need a clear understanding of what we mean by good.

Some readers may contend that there is no *real* meaning of good and that it is all "in the eye of the beholder." This attitude often takes the form of cultural relativism, the belief that good is whatever a particular society holds as good. When students, at the beginning of an ethics course, are asked what constitutes a right ethical action, a common response is that a right action is one that is approved of by "society." The judgment of society applies most notably to those things which are forbidden by law such as attacks on persons and property, or areas in which public opinion is strong such as marital infidelity, or rude and vulgar behavior. In areas in which there is no sanction by law or public opinion, the relativist notion of good may take the form of individual relativism called "subjectivism." Those who hold the subjectivist view assert that whatever you consider good *is* good for you and whatever I consider good *is* good for me. Good, in this view, depends solely on the wants and needs of the person who makes the judgment.

The relativist view, whether it is cultural or individual, has some acceptance in philosophy,[8] and seems to be supported by common experience. For example, in war each side believes that its cause embodies good and the enemy's cause embodies evil. Each may say with utter conviction, "God is on our side." The conflicting notion of what counts as good pervades all of the major controversies in society as well as the squabbles that bedevil everyday life. If the relativist view stands correct, then ethics has no role. Educators would serve young people better by teaching them to win whatever conflicts beset them, as students in law school learn to win their case whichever side they happen to be representing. Some might argue that all sides are equally good and therefore we should prefer "conflict resolution" or Win/Win rather than all-out conflict in which only one side wins. Those who hold this position may be right and they may be able to make a convincing argument for it. But such an argument depends on the premise that something really *is* better than something else. Otherwise, the advocates of conflict resolution have only a preference that is no better than those who contend that "winning is everything." The main task of ethics is to make a convincing case that the term "good" stands for something real and does not merely express subjective needs and wants.

Ordinary conversation equates good with whatever we desire. We must ask whether we call something good merely because we desire it or whether we have the capacity to recognize goodness that stands independently of what we happen to desire. The question is crucial to ethics because it marks the difference between a relativist view and a realist view. The relativist's view defines good as whatever anyone desires. The desires of the most foolish, ignorant, or even criminal person have as much standing as anyone else's. A further look at the question opens up the possibility of distinguishing between "desirable" and merely "desired."[9] By analogy, a clear distinction stands between "eaten" as in "the mushroom was eaten," and "edible." To say that it was eaten is a matter of fact. To say that it is or is not edible gives a guideline as to what the hungry person ought to do. Desires by themselves cannot serve as guides for action. Examples of misguided desires abound. Some people obviously desire to ingest harmful substances, to bet grocery money on slot machines, or to celebrate a sports victory by lighting fires in the street. We can obviously question the desirability of these actions. Is desirability just one person's opinion against another's? Or are some things really more desirable than others? My position holds that some things *really are* better than others, and their good quality makes them desirable. If this statement holds true, then we cannot rest on what we happen to desire and call it good, but need to find out what *is really* good so that we may learn to desire it.

Some people may not desire to hear this statement because it imposes an intellectual and moral demand that easygoing relativism does not. We may disagree with each other as to what is good, or even about the very meaning of good, but we have a basis to argue with each other and to work together to investigate controversial issues only if we can acknowledge the possibility of a real criterion for good.

How to Think about Ethical Questions

Ethical questions come up in ethical situations, and, in a sense, every situation is an ethical situation. Since we are always in a state of flux, any situation requires that we decide what action on our part, if any, might lead to improvement or deterioration. Everyday examples of ethical situations include getting out of bed in the morning, deciding what to eat during the day, choosing friends and associates, driving a car, reacting to other people's good or bad fortune, work habits, recreation, earning or preparing to earn a living, handling money, practicing a religion or not, identifying and pursuing long-range goals.

Books on ethics tend to ignore everyday situations, especially those that are not controversial, but since the situations call for action that brings about growth or deterioration, in large or small ways, we should approach them with the same principles by which we approach momentous and controversial problems. Some everyday decisions may seem trivial, but our everyday actions in each of these areas have a cumulative effect that is momentous for our lives and the lives of those close to us. As a much-quoted saying expresses it: "Sow an act and reap habit; sow a habit and reap a character; sow a character and reap a destiny."[10] Contemporary philosopher Tom Morris expressed a similar idea by stating that the most important thing he learned from all of his study of ethics is that when we perform any act, we are becoming the person that we are.[11]

In addition to the ethical situations that we encounter every day, there are other problems that are more obviously ethical situations because we have no consensus as to what is the best decision. These fill the contents of most courses in ethics and include dealing with: unwanted pregnancy, long and painful deaths, capital offenders, hunger and poverty, environmental deterioration, war and terrorism, pressure on business men and women to show a profit, pressure on politicians to win elections, and dislocations caused by a rapidly changing global economy.

When we deal with the everyday ethical situations as well as the socially controversial problems, we can think of ways to make ourselves better persons and create communities whose values and practices promote the good for all members of the community. The guide for making the best choice is the good understood as *teleological harmony*. Teleological in this case means that *unity* is the goal and intended outcome of the action. Unity shows itself as integrity, completeness, connectedness, and balance. An alternative term that we can use for teleological harmony is *purposive integration*.

When we attribute integrity to a person, we usually mean that the person is honest and trustworthy. These virtuous qualities reflect integrity, which literally means wholeness. Men and women of integrity *integrate* the many aspects of their characters, including their thoughts, words, actions, deepest wishes, long-range goals and their highest values. Integrity requires self-control over emotions and desires, as well as the ability to integrate with other individuals and communities.

Those who lack integrity allow various aspects of themselves to fly off in many directions; they *dis-integrate*. They may think one thing and say another, agree to one set of actions but perform others. They are unpredictable and, therefore, unreliable. Their emotions are out of control and their desire for immediate gratification impedes their own goals. Or their goals may be obsessive but out of line with what they claim to value. They see other people and communities as things to be used or obstacles to be dealt with.

The above descriptions of persons with and without integrity are two opposite types, and most of us fit somewhere in between. The ethical question asks which way we are moving. A good person spends a lifetime growing in integrity. Such people become better by making their lives more complete, more connected, and better balanced. The term teleological connotes that integrity is not an easily assumed fact, but rather a long-term goal.

Teleological harmony, which constitutes the meaning of a good individual, also defines a good society. Social harmony presents a challenge because individuals have a natural tendency to fear or hate anything or anyone foreign (fortunately, this is not our only natural tendency). Babies are often terrified by strange faces. Children form groups of friends who see other groups as their natural rivals on the streets or playgrounds. As adults, we form societies, but historically, other tribes or nations take on the role of enemies, especially if they have a different ethnicity, race, or religion. Even within a nation, foreigners are suspect, as are groups with differing lifestyles or ideologies.

The study of history can leave us with a sense of pessimism about the destiny of the human race. Recent history with horrifying events such as world wars, the holocaust, nuclear and fire bombings of civilian populations, mass murders in the old Soviet Union, in Africa and in Asia, can create a sense of doom and despair. Our hatreds are so strong that any hope for improvement seems illusory. The worst-case scenarios not only loom as real possibilities, but have too frequently become realities. Yet, the study of history also offers some hope. While doom is possible, it is not inevitable, and while moral progress is precarious, it does not constitute an impossible dream.

A look at some pessimistic predictions from the past can give us some perspective. In the early nineteenth century, many thoughtful Americans, as well as many more thoughtless ones, believed that a democratic government and way of life could not withstand the waves of Catholic immigrants. On another front, fights between workers and company owners were so brutal and deadly that the Marxian notion of all-out class warfare had some credence. Some Americans considered the notion of African-Americans taking an equal place in society as impossible, if not wrong, and many anti-equality proponents enforced their views with murder and oppression. The urban riots in the 1960s seemed to confirm the opinion of those whites and blacks who argued against the notion of a racially integrated society. Although the forces of divisiveness remain rampant, especially in politics, the fact that we as a nation avoided all-out labor wars and racial wars gives hope that we can overcome our current tendencies toward disintegration.

Harsh centrifugal forces have been even more violent on the international scale. For several decades, an all-out military showdown between the West and the Soviet Union, and between the West and the People's Republic of China, looked inevitable. At the time of this writing, Russia's invasion of Ukraine renews the dangers of the Cold War and even the possibility of nuclear war. But I contend that the period between 1945 and 1991 left less room for hope than the present. Time will show whether hope is warranted.

Today the fate of the Middle East and North Africa, and their relationship with the West, hangs in the balance. In addition, crimes against humanity continue to exist as realities and as threats. But looking at the world from our standpoint in the twenty-first century, a Roycean approach to differences would strive toward integrating all people within a society and all nations in an interdependent world of trade and cooperation. Good, as teleological harmony, emerges as the ethical guide for social as well as personal practice.

CHAPTER 2
The Neglected Concept of Loyalty

Learning to Distinguish Between Good and Evil

Because all of Royce's ideas cohere in an integrated whole, the initial understanding of anyone of them in isolation poses a problem. And yet, when we interpret Royce, we can only write or read one idea at a time. For this reason some repetition and recapitulation become necessary. In the above paragraphs, I have mentioned some of Royce's key ethical ideas, such as autonomy, duty, and loyalty, without much explication. In the following, I will try to clarify these and other key Roycean ethical ideas, especially the virtue of loyalty.

In all of Royce's major works dealing with ethical issues,[12] he presents his ideas as they develop through the struggles of life toward integrity or harmony rather than as eternal fully developed concepts superimposed on human life and conduct. Therefore, we can best understand his ethical principles by following the path of development. The most general and basic awareness of good consists in "whatever we regard as something to be welcomed, pursued, won, grasped, persisted in, preserved."[13] We experience or observe actions that signify the judgment that something is good in the response of small children to food that tastes good, young men and women pursuing their romantic interests, scientists testing hypotheses, artists uncovering beauty or truth, social activists working for what they believe is a more just society, and business men and women striving to make their enterprises profitable. The things that we call evil are those that we want to get rid of by removing them from ourselves or removing ourselves from them. Royce emphasizes that our actions of approach or avoidance show what we consider to be good and evil. Although the awareness of good and evil may include pleasure and pain, it is not limited to that sensual dichotomy. As Royce points out, we find the same dynamics of approach or avoidance "whether you regard us as animal or moralists, whether it is a sweet taste, a poem, a virtue, or God that we look to as good."[14]

Royce, as a psychologist, examines the complexity of human life that makes choosing good and evil problematic.[15] An adult trying to become more healthy and fit may see a fatty hamburger as tasting good but rejects it as bad in terms of nutrition; a hard workout may feel bad in terms of physical comfort, but is judged as good in terms of cardiovascular fitness. We discover the ambiguity of good and bad as small children. Parents and teachers tell us that some things we like are bad and the things we don't like are good. "Turn off the TV and do your homework." Our very sense of self develops through the interaction between our own impulses and "their rules."

We value our autonomy very highly and yet find it elusive. We are the center of so many conflicting impulses that we cannot even have a sense of autonomy unless we have some standard for weighing the relative value of each impulse. For example, a child may throw a temper tantrum or overindulge in junk foods in ways that he finds regrettable and embarrassing. A child has a better sense of personal autonomy and individuality when she freely chooses something that she and others perceive as her duty. "I did my homework." "I picked up my toys." The social environment which dictates some things as right and others as wrong, regardless of how we feel about them, provides a sense of duty, which aids in developing a hierarchy of goods and bads. We thereby learn to hate some of the things we do on our own impulse and love some things that we do in resistance to our impulse. But the desire for autonomy is strong and we resist the role of mere servants to someone else's rules. Royce finds harmony in the struggle between autonomy and duty in the virtue of loyalty.

Loyalty as the Cardinal Virtue

Royce argued that loyalty, if properly understood, can serve as the basis for all personal virtues and social principles. My purpose here is to make this idea clear and situate it in the twenty-first century. Royce stands virtually alone among seminal thinkers who proposed loyalty as the key to ethical thinking and living. One hundred years later the idea of loyalty, as well as most of Royce's philosophy, sits before us as a treasure, but mostly a buried treasure. The centrifugal forces of our time remind us of what W. B. Yeats wrote of Europe in 1919, in *The Second Coming*:

> Things fall apart; the center cannot hold
> Mere anarchy is loosed upon the world
> The blood-red tide is loosed.

We know that the quarter of a century following Yeats's poem did not end well and that the blood-red tide included the rise of totalitarian states, World War II, and the Holocaust. We don't know how our present crises will end, but the ideas of Royce could go a long way to leading us to a better landing.

Royce's idea of loyalty met with hostility in his time because critics saw loyalty as the cause of evil rather than its solution. After World War II and up to the present, loyalty can still be indicted as a cause of violence from the Nazi party, totalitarian regimes and countless other groups which committed atrocities and crimes in the name of loyalty.

Loyalty, in fact, can be used for evil, as can intelligence, bravery, discipline and ingenuity. Royce was aware of these problems and could articulate them at least as well as any of his critics. But he also had a solution, for which I will try to make a strong case. For those readers who might ask if the purpose of this book is to defend Royce's position rather than to provide a tool for ethical thinking, my answer is that the two go hand-in-hand. A person who can understand and appreciate

Royce's idea of loyalty will have a high-quality tool for dealing with ethical questions. Conversely, if these ideas serve well to deal with ethical questions, that very fact will confirm the value of Royce's ideas.

Royce offers *loyalty* as the virtue that best enables the individual to achieve personal integrity and leads to the integration of unique individuals in support of the common good. In its role as the supreme integrating force, loyalty nourishes and supports all of the virtues. By loyalty, Royce means *"The willing and practical and thoroughgoing devotion of a person to a cause."*[16] The central role of loyalty stems from the need that each individual has for an integrating power. In isolation, each human being consists of many competing biological, psychological, and social forces and needs. To become individuals, we turn to something that we consider larger than ourselves, which gives us meaning, purpose, and identity. In short, the cause enables us to become an integrated self.

Because loyalty to a cause constitutes a necessary factor for our very personhood, it stands as a universal need. While some people may stumble through life without devotion to anything, most of us will seek and hopefully find a cause that enables us to organize the conflicting aspects of our organic nature into an integrated self. An immediate problem emerges in the fact that many people adhere to evil causes. These include such things as tyrannical governments, violent religious sects, racist ideologies, criminal organizations, and street gangs. These realities would indicate that loyalty, far from standing as the basis for virtue and morality, is actually an evil aspect of human nature.

Distinguishing Good and Bad Loyalty

Royce answers that the distinction between good and bad loyalty can be found in the very need for loyalty. Since each person experiences the need for a cause, any cause that the person adopts will appear to that person as good, even a cause that is objectively evil. When individuals find a cause that enables them to overcome the confusion and narrowness of their isolated egos, they will cherish that cause above all other goods. Therefore, the worst thing that you can do to a person is to destroy that person's cause, and the best thing that you can do is to promote his or her cause. A cause that destroys another's cause is to that extent evil, a cause that promotes another's cause is, in this regard, good. A morally good person will not only be loyal to his or her own cause, but will choose a cause that promotes rather than destroys the beloved cause of others. Royce defines the ability to respect other people's causes as "loyalty to loyalty," which becomes the guiding principle for evaluating all moral actions and virtues.

The phrase "loyalty to loyalty" has not made its way into our common discourse. It does not show up as a leading idea in ethics books and courses. In fact, it does not show up at all, except in scholarly works on Josiah Royce that are read mainly by other Royce scholars. In this book I hope to remedy that unfortunate neglect by showing that the idea of loyalty to loyalty is both accessible to everyone and very useful for approaching ethical problem and nourishing the good.

In the above paragraphs I tried to show that loyalty to a cause supports autonomy by allowing a person to integrate her impulses into an order that presents desires as better or worse. Loyalty also allows the autonomous individual to obey a duty to something larger than himself. Further, it nourishes the good as teleological harmony by joining many persons into a single unity of life. Loyalty to loyalty frees the groups, centered around loyalty to specific causes, from a separation and hostility to other groups. When we are loyal to loyalty, we not only respect a cause that is not our own, but we "secure the greatest possible increase in loyalty."[17]

The notion of the greatest increase in loyalty may seem abstract and hard to apply, but an example will help. The First Amendment to the Constitution of the United States provides such an example, although I am not aware that Royce himself ever used it to illustrate this point. Part of the Amendment states that "Congress shall make no law respecting the establishment of religion or prohibiting the free exercise thereof." The principle behind this amendment is generally referred to as the separation of church and state. Some Americans are passionately loyal to their religious faith, and others just as ardent in their agnostic or atheist world-view. This fundamental disagreement on the meaning of life can and often does lead to conflict and disharmony. But what if people on all sides of the issue were loyal to the principle that each of us ought to be free to follow our belief without interference? This attitude would not only teach us to respect each other's beliefs and loyalties, but would also integrate all of us into a society that respects universal human rights. Such, of course, was the intention of the framers of the Bill of Rights.

Other examples of conflicting loyalties are examined in this book. The examples include some of the very thorny and stubborn conflicts dealing with the economy, the environment, abortion, euthanasia, and capital punishment. Although there may be right and wrong answers among various proposed solutions to these conflicts, the deeper problem involves conflicting loyalties. Loyalty to loyalty does not offer any quick or easy solutions, but it does offer a way to proceed. Articulating this procedure constitutes the task of this book.

We can now sum up the relation among Royce's three central ethical categories, autonomy, duty, and goodness. Autonomy as self-direction would seem to favor an individualistic approach to ethics. In extreme, it might lead to a subjectivism in which each person becomes the measure of what is right or wrong. This mentality found expression in the 1960s in the lifestyle of some young people and song lyrics such as "It's my life and I'll throw it away if I want to." Duty, by contrast would seem to favor the collective, and impose binding ties on the individual. We can think of the soldier committing atrocities because he was "obeying orders," or the "organization man" in business doing whatever he is told in the name of profit. But Royce held to both autonomy and duty and rejected both individualism and collectivism. The balance comes through the third category of good as teleological harmony, expressed ethically as loyalty to loyalty. Autonomous individuals freely choose causes that impose a duty but which respect their own autonomy and that of everyone else. It is precisely in our loyal relations with the community that we find our own unique task that we autonomously choose. As Royce says of loyalty: "It is a universally human good. For it is simply the finding of a harmony of self and the world, - such a harmony as can alone content any human being."[18] Loyalty to loyalty, therefore, leads to a community of unique and autonomous individuals.

Four Questions to Aid Ethical Interpretation

The following chapters develop the theme of teleological integration, and apply it to ethical situations that surround friendship and community, love and sex, business, the beginning of life, the end of life, social and economic imbalances, work and play, and living in a consumerist society. In each of these we will tease out the ethical implications of situations by asking a few penetrating questions. This list is not exhaustive and you may find other questions that can also help clarify an ethical situation. These questions flow from the description presented in this chapter. A brief explanation serves as a review of some of the key ideas.

Questions 1: *What is desirable as opposed to merely desired?* We can distinguish between an outcome that is desired and one that is desirable. The term "desired" simply expresses the fact that someone desires the object in question. The object might be desired by one person or by nearly everybody. But the mere fact of being desired does not indicate whether fulfilling the object is good. A person may desire to eat a mushroom found in the woods, have one more beer, or do physical harm to a person whom he finds obnoxious. But to say that something is desirable means that we would desire it if we knew all of the consequences. We will relate this question in each context to the positive or negative impact on teleological harmony.

Question 2: *How can we best enhance our personal integrity as well as that of other persons and our integration with each other?* This question explores good as the teleological harmony. Actions are good to the extent that they lead to well-integrated persons living in a well-integrated society.[19] Integrity as a characteristic of us as persons means that our words are true to our beliefs, and our actions are true to our most cherished values. We promote integration when we do what is in our power to give everyone a place in the various communities that we share as well as in the larger society. We achieve personal integrity through the virtue of loyalty, which unites our desires, passions, and energy in service to our cause. We promote social integration through the larger virtue of loyalty to loyalty, which guides our personal loyalty to work for the universal harmony of all goods. Loyalty to a cause enables us to integrate our own conflicting desires into a consistent pattern of action, and as Royce points out loyalty nourishes the things that we ordinarily call virtues, things such as honesty, fairness, benevolence, and respect. As Royce says the aim of loyalty is a "united harmonious devotion, not to various conflicting causes, but to one system of causes, and so to one cause."[20] Since we choose our causes, we can deliberately choose those that lead to the universal spread of loyalty.

Question 3. *How would we treat each person if we felt positive respect and affection for them?* To treat a person with respect means to recognize their personhood and not regard them as either mere instruments or obstacles to your own purposes. German philosopher Immanuel Kant (1724–1804) defined the unconditional imperative, "Treat each person as an end also, never merely as a means." When we meet persons whom we respect because of their position or achievements, we tend to treat them with our best behavior; we would not think of deceiving them, insulting them, or in any way harming or "disrespecting" them. Ethical behavior flows naturally when we remember that every person is deserving of respect. We might not be able to feel affection toward everyone, but we can treat each person the way we treat people whom we care about. We can treat each person so as to contribute to his or her spiritual growth. In symmetrical relation, we can follow the golden rule, which is taught in some form by every world religion, "Treat others as you would have them treat you."

When relationships are not symmetrical because of a difference of gender, age, or status, we can treat people the way we want those whom we love to be treated. For example, sexual harassment in the workplace would not be a problem if every male employer treated women employees the way he should want his wife, mother, or daughter to be treated. We ought to treat children and young people the way we want our sons and daughters to be treated, and older people the way we want our parents and grandparents to be treated. In Royce's philosophy, our attitude toward each person is enlightened and fortified by a sense of loyalty and of "reverence for the relations of life." [21]

Question 4: *How may we use moral imagination in each situation to nourish the good of teleological harmony?* Moral imagination means realizing that the distinction between right and wrong is necessary but not sufficient. Ethical living means nourishing the good, and that involves searching for answers that lead the whole community toward teleological harmony. Josiah Royce held that logical thinking ought to have *uberty,* which means the full-breasted richness of life. Our thinking ought to nourish the good as a mother nourishes her young. Any thinking, especially imaginative thinking that nourishes teleological harmony is good ethical thinking.

In summary, the questions that we will ask in each section are:

1. What is desirable as opposed to merely desired?

2. How can you best enhance your personal integrity as well as that of other persons, and your integration with each other?

3. How would you treat each person in the situation if you felt positive respect and affection for them?

4. How may we use moral imagination in this situation to nourish teleological harmony?

CHAPTER 3

The Self as an Ethical Task

Royce's Teleological Approach

As stated in the opening chapter, this book takes a *teleological* approach to ethics. The term teleological stems from the word *telos* meaning end, purpose, or fulfillment. In deciding what is the right thing to do, we look at the end, the purpose, the intention of our chosen course of action. While there are older and better-known teleological theories such as those of Aristotle and St. Thomas, Josiah Royce's notion of good as "teleological harmony" will permeate this book. Royce's approach to ethics can be situated in the context of teleological theories by comparing him to Aristotle, the father of teleology.

Aristotle begins his Nicomachaen Ethics by describing the "end." [22] He argues that an archer cannot begin to shoot unless he knows the target. The Greek word *telos* should become part of everyone's ethical and personal vocabulary. It is often translated as "end," not in the sense of demise, but in the sense of a goal. As developed by Aristotle, *telos* also connotes personal development in the sense of actualizing one's potential. A student actualizes his or her potential to become, say, a nurse, doctor, accountant, teacher, lawyer, business leader, mechanic, or full-time parent. As we perform acts of beneficence, honesty, courage, diligence, and loyalty, we develop good habits, called virtues, which enable us to actualize our potential to be beneficent, honest, brave, diligent and loyal. Knowing what we want to become, what potential we want to actualize, serves as an indispensable tool for knowing how to act day in and day out.

For Royce, teleological harmony constitutes the purpose of every *idea* that we try to fulfill, the *life-plan* by which we create our very selves, and the *loyal acts* that build human community. [23] We will take a closer look at each of these components; *idea, life plan,* and *loyal act.* The word "idea" has several meanings, all of which connote a state of consciousness. Some philosophers have used the term idea to mean any image presented to the mind such as "blue" or "cold." In this book I use the term "idea" in Royce's sense of a state of mind that involves a proposed course of action regarding the object. For example, the mere awareness of blue or cold does not constitute an idea. But homeowners may have an *idea to paint the trim of their house blue*; a sense of being cold may *instigate the idea of putting on a sweater*. The purposeful act is part of the idea, and the idea is fulfilled with the completion of the action.[24] This notion of an idea takes on special importance for ethics since ethics involves doing and promoting good rather than just feeling or thinking about it. We can define every idea as teleological because we find the meaning of an idea in the purpose which the idea intends.

Our *life plan* plays an essential role in our very personhood. The meaning of our life depends on teleology. Often, we hear the terms such as "the human person" and "the individual," and may think of them as given, as ready-made objects. But in reality, we each begin our life with potential, and as long as we are alive, some of our potential remains unfulfilled. Our "self" does not emerge ready-made like Venus from the head of Zeus. For each of us, our *self* presents a task to be completed. We create our selves by finding a cause or purpose to live for and by developing a life plan to reach that fulfillment.[25] We are not limited to a single cause. Our cause may in fact be a system of causes that cooperate in promoting loyalty to loyalty. We may choose well or badly, wisely or foolishly, for life or for death. The study of ethics intends to make each person a better judge of what constitutes a good choice. The burden of making the actual choice falls on each of us.

Finally, while ethics permeates our individual destinies, it also has rich social dimensions and requires acts of loyalty. Each of us depends on the various communities to which we belong for everything, from our bodily life to our psychological well-being to our deepest spiritual meanings. While we depend on community, community also depends on us. Our ideas and our life plans can help to build or destroy communities. The ethical judgment of all that we do depends on our intended impact, not only on our own lives, but the lives of others and to the communal structures on which we all depend.

Potential as the Key to Ethical Understanding

While each of us is a work-in-progress, we are not blank slates. Some empiricist philosophers described the mind as *tabula rasa,* or blank slate. This makes a poor metaphor because reality does not write ideas on passive minds. Rather, we actively develop ideas as we interact with our environment. For example, the fifteen-month-old toddler approaching a step down may create the idea that she is less likely to fall if she turns backward and crawls down. The complex idea of turning around and crawling was not written on her mind by experience; she had to conceive the idea to prevent the unpleasant experience from ever happening. The same dynamic takes place in the most sophisticated adult thinking in science, business, healthcare, education, or anything else. The potentiality of our mind does not imply blankness and passivity, but rather a specific power. "Potential" stems from the Latin word for power, *potentia.* The Greek word used by Aristotle, *dynamis,* provides such English words as dynamo and dynamite. We can learn to make better decisions on what we make of our lives by looking at our capabilities, our potential.

What can we know about the potential of each human person and specifically the person that we call our "self?" The answer to this question requires that we find out what we can know about human beings in general, and the more difficult question of what we can each know about our particular selves.

Our ethical beliefs and actions depend on our beliefs about the meaning of human existence. Beliefs about our nature develop over history as we live and encounter problems and opportunities in our physical and social environments. Storytellers, philosophers and, later in history, psychologists, scientists, politicians, and media pundits contribute to the formulation of the beliefs that we share in common. Each of us learns in our particular environment, our shared environment, and our successful and unsuccessful attempts to thrive. Traditional teleological theories took human nature as a given. Our task was to know what it means to be a human person so that we could work toward becoming a good person.

Royce emphasized the uniqueness of each individual, and therefore the unique end of each of us. Our goal is self-determined by choosing the cause to which we pledge our loyalty. But the quest to become a person can be enhanced by looking at a traditional approach to this question. This approach is not offered as an alternative, or as part of a menu of alternatives, but as a set of insightful ideas that can enhance the Roycean ideas presented here. The following beliefs about the nature of being human have developed over time and express general truths.

Human nature includes those characteristics that we share with all animals. Ancient and medieval philosophers defined us as rational animals. While the notion of what this means has changed over time, the reality of our animal nature has certain constancies, especially our mortality. Because we are going to die, our life is precarious and limited. Awareness of vulnerability can awaken us to the obligation to treat ourselves and all others with the utmost respect. Our time and our life are precious. We can learn to see that time quickly slips away and that missed opportunities constitute moral problems. In dealing with other people, we would treat them with greater care if we thought they were going to die. In fact, they are going to die. *This awareness increases our moral burden but also releases our moral energy.*

Awareness of personal mortality underlines the human need for loyalty. Those who live for their own individual pleasure or power inevitably meet defeat as death takes away their perceived goods. In contrast to the individualists whose insatiable desire for pleasure or power meets frustration, Royce depicts the meaning of mortality for the loyal:

> They, too, are indeed subject to fortune; their loyalty, also, is an insatiable passion to serve their cause; they also know what it is to meet with tasks that are too vast for mortals to accomplish. Only their very loyalty, since it is a willing surrender of the self to the cause, is no hopeless warfare with this fate but is a joyous acceptance in advance of the inevitable destiny of every individual human being.[26]

The person who lives loyally for a cause can live and die in the hope that the cause endures.

In addition to mortality, our animal nature requires that we obtain food and other necessities, that we watch out for our health and safety and that of our neighbor, and that we reproduce sexually and take care of our young. In later chapters we will investigate each of these human needs with the suggestion how they may be met while nourishing the good.

While we humans have much in common with other animals, reason is our defining characteristic. The classical definition of humans as rational animals does not depict us as mere animals but rather emphasizes the qualification of *rational* animal. Writers and teachers often make reference to reason without stopping to say what it is. Reason may be something so familiar to us that it needs no introduction. But since the term is so often used and misused, readers have the right to know what each writer means by reason. Reason consists of the ability to form concepts so that we can be aware of things that are not present to our senses. It goes beyond memory and imagination in that we are not limited to pictures of things, but may also form logical and mathematical connections by which we unite things into greater and greater generalizations. Our rationality provides us with a desire to learn and to find or create meaning in our world. We need to find a way to connect the rich variety of experiences into a whole, or at least into a manageable number of parts. Without such connections or meanings, experience would overwhelm us. In the words of William James, it would be a "big, buzzing, blooming, confusion."[27]

Royce defines reason as "the power to see widely, and steadily, and connectedly."[28] He illustrates the meaning of reason by showing the distinction between a reasonable and an unreasonable person. In ordinary language, when we consider a person to be unreasonable, we usually mean that the person sees only one side of an issue or one aspect of a problem. Or if the unreasonable person sees several things, he does not see the connections between them or does not think consistently. Such a person might have one set of standards for him or herself and another set for everyone else. The reasonable man or woman sees as many sides of an issue as possible and sees them as a whole and how they develop over time. By rationally connecting our experiences, we can form ideas about how to live our lives personally and in cooperation with other people. Reason gives us the desire and the ability to deliberately seek goals and to find ways to live with others justly and beneficially.

Our nature as rational animals connotes mortality and rationality. But other qualities that spring from our nature endow us with a sense of community, freedom, creativity, and the potential to be something more. First, we can depict ourselves and our neighbors as social animals. Like many animals, we like to live together. But our rationality expands our sociality beyond our immediate tribe. We belong to many interlocking communities, ultimately including the human race and, in fact, the whole biosphere. We depend on these communities and they depend on us. This awareness provides us with moral guidance on how we play our many roles to the benefit of ourselves and our community.

Freedom and Creativity

Freedom implies creativity. We can exercise freedom only if the possible futures outnumber the eventual outcomes. If there are two choices, as when we come to a fork in the road or find ourselves torn between two career paths or two job offers, we have a degree of freedom. But freedom can sometimes be much richer than merely choosing among the given options. We can sometimes view the future as malleable and we can imagine real possibilities that had not previously occurred to us. Such a view greatly expands our freedom. We can, to some degree, shape our reality. Of course, reality does not yield to all of our desires and ideas, but it might yield to some. We can see the malleability of reality by looking at the work of creative people from artists and scientists to business founders and nation builders. We can find the limits of our own creativity only by testing them.

The creative potential of each human person presents a source of hope and even exhilaration, but also imposes a moral duty. We have the psychological *and* moral need to take part in meaningful work that carries on the process of creation. Failure to do so constitutes what traditional moral writers called "sloth" or laziness. More recently, psychiatrist and spiritual writer Scott Peck called laziness the "original sin" because it prevents us from achieving our purpose in life.[29]

We can enrich our understanding of Royce's insights on creativity by comparing his view to that of Charles S. Peirce, whom Royce credited for his own philosophical development. Royce named the universal beloved community as his moral ideal. An explanation of Royce's idea of community will be presented at the end of this chapter. The comparison with Peirce, presented here, will help make Royce's idea more accessible. Peirce identified the highest norm as "concrete reasonableness." By this term he meant the continuing inclusion of real events in ever larger generalizations. The modifier "concrete" signals that Peirce did not mean mere abstractions or "airy nothings." Examples of concrete reasonableness include biological evolution, in which molecules gain complexity and integration, as well as the Gospel of John, which teaches universal love. Peirce expressed his view of the creation of the world and the part that we humans play:

> The creation of the universe, which did not take place during a certain busy week in 4004 B. C., but is going on today and never will be done, is this very development of reason... Under this conception, the ideal of conduct will be to exercise our little function in the operation of creation by giving a hand toward rendering the world more reasonable whenever, as the slang is, it is up to us.[30]

This insight of Peirce on taking a role in creation as the ideal of conduct expresses the same thought that Royce had on creativity and one that presents a leading ethical idea for us.

Royce offers a very fertile ground for creative thinking in the process of interpretation. While traditional philosophy offered percepts and concepts as the two ways of knowing, Royce, following Charles S. Peirce, emphasized interpretation as a third and most important way of knowing.[31] *Interpretation consists of a mind revealing the meaning of a sign to another mind.* A sign can be anything that has meaning, for example, a traffic signal, a spoken or written sentence, a painting, a facial expression, or a cloud formation. We find the prototype and most common expression of interpretation in a language translator. The translator reveals the meaning of, say, a Russian novel to an English-speaking reader. The English translation becomes a new sign, which a literature professor interprets for her students. The professor's lecture becomes a new sign and the process can go on indefinitely.

The two minds need not be two separate people. We often engage in the interpretative process when thinking in solitude. Royce describes this as the future self-interpreting for the past self, or the aspect of a person that is coming into being to the aspect of the self that previously exists. For example, a student of language may be using his new skill and knowledge to interpret a foreign phrase to his old monolingual self.

Royce sees interpretation as the key to great world-changing creativity in science, religion, and art. Every creative thought begins with percepts and concepts but must go further by the act of interpretation. He cites Charles Darwin who interpreted the rich data yielded by naturalistic observation. The beginning of interpretation consists of comparing and contrasting. The creative insight comes about by discovering a third principle that enables the interpreter to unify the contrasting data. In Darwin's case, the work of the economist Thomas Malthus on competition in human populations led Darwin to the principle of natural selection. This principle enabled him to show the connection of the fossil record with living creatures and thereby to explain not only the development but even the origin of species. [32]

Ranging from naturalistic science to prophetic religion, Royce shows that the same dynamic that worked in Darwin's case also presented itself in the prophet Amos. The prophet contrasted religious beliefs and practices of sacrificial religion with the plight of the poor and the indifference and injustice of the people. Amos introduced the idea of "God who delights not in sacrifices but in righteousness." This idea of God changed both religion and morality by bringing the two together as a unified ethico-religious insight. [33]

Creativity through interpretation applies not only to the world-changing works of prophets, artists and scientists, but also to the growth and development of each person.[34] As stated above, we begin life, not as a unified self, but as a meeting ground of many, often conflicting, drives, desires, and ideas.

We have many ideas, which may or may not stand in some obvious relation to each other by way of contrast or agreement. The work of uniting the self consists of integrating conflicting or estranged ideas into a meaningful whole. We can take the first step in this process by an act of deliberate comparison. Comparison, by itself, does not provide an integrated unity. Integration requires a new idea that unites the two seemingly unrelated ideas. Royce affirms that "for this act, originality and sometimes even genius is required." [35] The "new idea" refers to what Charles S. Peirce called "a third," an interpreter. As in the example above, a linguist who translates one language into another is a "third," an interpreter.

Royce gives several examples to illustrate this point, from specialized mathematics to art and poetry. But I will offer an example from the moral development of an individual. A young person may hold a strong sense of self and desire to flourish in her personal and professional life. At the same time, she may have a nagging sense of social responsibility and feel the need to help others. The dichotomy between egoism and altruism looms before her. But the "third idea," in this case, is loyalty. The loyal person is not selfless but rather has a strong sense of self. The more self she has, the more she can contribute to her cause. Her work in promoting the cause in turn strengthens her personal development. Royce summarizes the relation between our individual and social sense in his answer to the question of whether we have duties to ourselves:

> "Yes, precisely in so far as I have the duty to be actively loyal at all. For loyalty needs not only a willing but also an active servant. My duty to myself is, then, the duty to provide my

cause with one who is strong enough and skillful enough to be effective according to my own natural powers. [36]

Royce includes among these powers, the care of health, self-cultivation, self-control, and spiritual power. His exemplar of the loyal person was Ida Lewis, the lighthouse keeper whose strength and boating skill saved many shipwrecked sailors from drowning.

The relationship between a strong individual and well-developed sense of social responsibility applies to any man or woman in business, healthcare, education, politics, science, art, or any profession. To cite some examples, you cannot become a better teacher, physical therapist, or home-construction tradesman without enhancing the good of students, clients, or home owners. Persons who are loyal to the purpose of their professions may see them as causes and not merely jobs. The loyal person flourishes personally and contributes to the common good. Becoming a fully integrated person requires the creative act of bringing opposing forces into harmony.

Human creativity carries several important ethical ramifications, all of which can be enhanced by a clear understanding of interpretation. One of the key aspects of creativity that life presents to all of us is "moral imagination." Life often presents dilemmas in which we have to choose between two goods or between two evils. Ordinary thought may direct us to choose the greater good or the lesser evil. Or there may be a clear choice between right and wrong, but the "right" choice leads to a lot of harm or sacrifices a lot of good. Sometimes reality limits us to one of two choices. But now and then our moral imagination may happily reveal three, four, or many possible paths. Moral imagination should permeate the discussion of every ethical issue. For example, suppose a child commits an infraction of his parents' rules shortly before an important opportunity, such as a field trip or a summer camp that means a lot to the child. A parent may feel trapped between ignoring the infraction and taking away a good learning opportunity for the child. It might not occur to the distressed parent, caught up in the situation, that there are ways to teach the child that his infraction was a bad decision without taking away a good life experience. A satisfactory study of ethics will encourage the student to look for ways not only to choose the better of two decisions but also to exercise moral imagination to enhance the good.

Royce's notions of interpretation and loyalty provide a way to train moral imagination. Interpretation always involves the mediation of a *third term* that bridges the gap between two terms, as a translator is the third term who bridges the gap between a language and person who does not know the language. In the example given above, of the offending child and the offended parent, the parent himself can be the mediator between his own offended self and the child. If he is able to step back and take the position of mediator, he will take care to correct the offending behavior in a way that benefits the child and does not damage the parent-child relationship. The same dynamic applies to any relationship between unequal parties such as employer-employee, or teacher-student, or between equal partners such as spouses, friends, or adult siblings. In each case loyalty to the good of the family, the educational process, the workplace, or the friendship enables a person to overcome the dangerous and destructive relationship of two angry or hurt individuals.

Taking the role of mediator both requires and trains moral imagination whether the mediator is one of the two parties stepping back and taking the role of a third person, or an actual third person such as a mutual friend or a counselor. *Imagination*, which Royce saw as one of the leading teachers of loyalty, enables the third person to see what the relationship could be, a vision that is likely to be blurred if not erased in the heat of the immediate conflict. Closely allied to imagination as a teacher of loyalty is *sorrow* for the loss of what had been.[37] Remembering the love, the friendship, the good times, can reignite the awareness of what could be. If the loss is irreversible, sorrow can motivate a person to reconfigure relationships to avoid or at least minimize future harm.

Loyalty to loyalty evokes the duty to seek mediation in every conflict. An attitude of respect for people with whom we disagree, enhanced by recognition of their loyalty to a cause, enriches our own understanding of the good as teleological harmony. Such respect may enable us to see the good in the other's cause to which we might have been blind. Increased insight may also awaken us to a weakness in our own perception of reality. For example, the task of ethics involves interpreting the pro-life position on abortion, and euthanasia to a pro-choice person, and the pro-choice position to a pro-life person. A pro-life advocate might be insensitive to the plight of women with unwanted pregnancies, and a pro-choice person can fail to appreciate the reality of prenatal life. Although the two sides may never agree on the morality of abortion, a softening of positions may lead each to care about the mother and the unborn child in ways that are more conducive to a better life for each.

Other conflicts that interpretation can help to heal are between environmental and industrial interests, and between libertarians and social justice advocates. All the social divisions that we face on issues such as capital punishment, immigration, the environment, the economy, and health care, can be alleviated through mediation rather than by politicians posturing with winner–take-all stances. Mediation may not solve the problems or end the divisions, but it will move our understanding forward better than the ethical doctrines that see their own side as right and the other as wrong.

The Beloved Community

From a Roycean point of view we achieve the highest potential for each individual and for our society by practicing a thorough-going devotion to a fully integrated community. Ethics requires us each to strive to create a self who devotes his or her life to a chosen cause that contributes in a unique individual way to the ultimate human integration that Royce called "The Beloved Community."

A better understanding of the meaning of the "Universal Beloved Community" requires a grasp of Royce's notion of any community. A mere crowd or collection of persons does not constitute a community. There are several conditions for a genuine community, one that is necessary for developing unique and free individuals. A community comes about as a temporal process involving interpretation so that the individuals understand the meaning of the community and their place within it. Since communities develop in time, a community must have a past. It must have a more or less conscious history, real or ideal, and this history is part of its very essence.

Second, it must have a future that consists of shared hopes and expectations. The community consists of a number of distinct individuals, each with a distinctive past and set of aspirations, who engage in mutual communication among themselves. The extended pasts and futures of members include some events that are identical, and each member has a loyal love of the community.[38]

The term "beloved community" refers to the community that rescues the individual from alienation. It comes to him as a free gift, a grace, and saves him from desolation. Of course, small groups such as gangs or cults can give the isolated individual the sense of belonging and being saved. But tendencies toward disintegration persist. Antagonisms arise between individuals, between individuals and the community, and between warring communities. Individual struggles with conflicting loyalties may be thrown back on to conflicting motives within themselves. In order to achieve genuine integrity of self, the individual needs a loyalty to a community that overcomes all divisions. We do not find such a community in the visible world, but we can know the ideal and integrate our lives by loyally working toward it.

The Universal Community is the ideal unity of all humans in a Beloved Community. Every act that Royce, following Peirce, calls "interpretation" brings two divided ideas together and unites them into a higher unity. As this process goes on in our finite world, it moves us toward the universal beloved community. In our natural dealing with other people, we have feelings of hate as well as love for individuals and for the communities of which we are a part. This ambiguity holds even for our own lives. We may love our life or feel a sense of discontent and disappointment toward it. For us to develop a permanent steady unbroken love for our community we need to receive the love as a gift from something higher. Royce explains that, in Christian terminology, this would be expressed as a grace from God. While Royce sees historical Christianity as an example of this gift of community, he contends that the idea is larger than Christianity or any historical religion and expresses a universal human doctrine of life. Whatever name we give to the higher being, or if we leave it nameless, we can still experience the senses of love for the community as a gift.

In developing this idea, Royce uses the startling phrase "falling in love with the universe." This term connotes that reality consists of something worthy of our love and devotion as opposed to being just dead matter. The notion of a lovable universe means that we can interpret our own attempts at harmony within our individual selves, within our communities of history and hope, and among all communities, as working parts of a universal beloved community. Such an outlook allows for the greatest possibility of fulfilling the ethical task of creating an integrated self.

CHAPTER 4
Friendship, Love, and Personal Development

The previous chapter emphasized the idea that human personhood is not something given, but a task to be achieved. Of course, the human organism has the potential to be a person and to exhibit the qualities discussed in the previous chapter, qualities such as reason, free will, communal sense, freedom, and creativity. But personhood comes about through interaction between the individual organism and society with all of its supports and constraints. Each of us comes into the world with a myriad of drives, needs, and desires. Apart from social training we would each remain a collection of diverse and conflicting characteristics that would fail to constitute an identity. The entire process of becoming a person consists of a lifelong interplay between the individual and society.

Throughout Royce's work, he emphasizes that the ethical task of human life requires us to integrate a multiplicity of conflicting drives in order to create a "self." In Royce's words:

> We are naturally creatures of wavering and conflicting motives, passions, and desire. The supreme aim of life is to triumph over this natural chaos, to set some plan of life above all others to give unity to our desires, to organize our activities, to win... the strength of spirit which is above the narrowness of each one of our separate passions.[39]

The development of our selves involves not only integrating our internal motives, passions and desires but also integrating each of our selves with an ever-expanding community. These are not two separate tasks to be done in tandem, but rather, two aspects of the same task of integration. Loyalty to a cause, as described in chapter 1, not only joins us with other selves who share our cause, but it also enables us to unify our own lives making them focused and stable. [40]

This chapter will present the development of a person in terms of personal friendship, love, and sex. Later chapters will deal with the business world, the larger society, and the natural environment. Personal development in each of these dimensions deals with integrity and coincides with ethical development.[41]

We can improve our thinking on the ethical implications of relationships by applying the questions listed at the end of Chapter 1. The term "friendship" in the summary questions will be used to denote all positive relationships including what we usually call "love relationships."

1. What is desirable as opposed to merely desired in our friendships?

2. How can we best enhance our personal integrity as well as that of our friends?

3. How would we treat each friend if we felt positive respect and affection for them and were not merely attracted to them for pleasure or usefulness?

4. How may we use moral imagination in this situation to nourish the good of our friends as well as the friendship itself?

The Journey to Maturity

As you read the following account of personal development, you may want to compare it to how you personally experienced coming of age. How is this account similar to your life and how is it different? What aspects do you agree with and which do you disagree with? What specific memories in your life confirm or run contrary to what is presented here?

The following discussion does not derive directly from Royce, but expresses a contemporary account compatible with his views. We begin life as animals, human animals, but animals nevertheless. As babies we can care only about our immediate organic needs: food, the pleasure of human touch, comfort, the sound of a voice, and freedom from loud noises. But as soon as we can recognize another person, the face and voice of our parents, we begin our journey from purely organic feeling, through ego-awareness, to maturity as members of the human community. But this journey presents such difficulties, that many find it easier to go off the path or to stop somewhere along the way.[42]

Our personal development and our growing sense of community go hand-in-hand; it is impossible to develop one without the other. By the age of two we recognize our parents as being other people and we rise in full rebellion against them. At least we would if we did not love them and acknowledge our complete dependence on them. Learning to live means reconciling our parents' rules and demands with our own budding sense of autonomy. Siblings stand out as our natural rivals as well as our first friends. In our interaction with them, we first begin to define who we are and of what our role in the family consists. Outside the family we usually find playmates and most often prefer same-sex playmates. Our first awareness of the other sex is that they are "the other," different and unappealing. For both boys and girls there is a need for acceptance among our playmates as well as rivalry and fighting. We see ourselves in our playgroups and want to be part of the group. But our playmates are also seen as the "others" who threaten us physically or psychologically. Group identification is very strong and, as we grow, concordance with our group becomes a strong determiner of what we consider right and wrong.[43] The group may be a sports team, a school class, a scout troop, a religious education class, or a street gang.

For better and for worse, the attitude toward the other sex changes in early adolescence. (In our modern society, life would be easier for parents and teachers if the hormones remained dormant until sometime after twenty.) But recognition of the other sex happens. At first the attraction is mixed with the antagonism of childhood. Male and female chauvinists among heterosexuals are people whose growth stopped at an early adolescent level. Desire for the other sex is mostly if not exclusively physical, and the cute girl or boy emerges as at least a potential object of pleasure. For homosexuals the attitude toward members of their own sex changes.

In late adolescence and early adulthood, most of us develop special friendships that are same-sex but not sexual. The best friend embodies some of the qualities that we most admire, whether or not we ourselves possess these qualities. Friendship involves our mutual self-recognition in the other. Without the friend we would not perceive the personal qualities that we possess or yearn to possess. My friend and I experience a mutual self-recognition, and my world is no longer limited to the exclusive egoism of childhood. Relationship with the other sex no longer limits itself to physical desire but now includes a strong erotic dimension as well as the possibility of real friendship between men and women. A heterosexual relationship constitutes a mutual self-recognition of the androgynous human. The term "androgynous" is from the Greek words for man and woman and connotes that neither is complete without the other. In Plato's dialogue *Symposium*, the dramatist Aristophanes tells how Zeus had split our ancestors in half in response to rebellion. Now we must each find our other half to become a complete person. In Aristophanes' account, sometimes the "other half" is of the same sex. In this case the androgynous qualities are found in each individual.

Friendship and the Good

All friendship consists of seeing good in the one we call our friend. It might be helpful, before developing the idea of friendship in Roycean terms, to look at the clear structure of good and its relationship to being in the Aristotelian tradition. Aristotle distinguished three kinds of friendship based on three different kinds of good; the pleasant, the useful, and the good in itself.[44] We call something good if it is pleasant, as when we say something tastes good or feels good. Sometimes we consider people friends because they are fun to be with. Aside from the particular pleasure that a person might give, our animal nature makes it more pleasant for most people to run in packs than to be alone. As Aristotle said, "For without friends, no one would choose to live, though he had all other goods."[45] This desire for a pack of friends is especially strong in childhood and adolescence but continues through life. In the context of pleasant goods, a boy-girl relationship might be based on nothing more than mutual pleasure.

Aristotle defines, as a second kind of good, that which is useful, whether or not it is pleasant. We can think of such examples as a good investment, a good solution to a problem, a good test. Sometimes we call persons friends because they are useful, whether or not they happen to be pleasant. Examples might include a friend who can do a certain kind of work, a friend who can get Steeler tickets, a friend who can arrange a job interview. In marital relationships the useful person might be the trophy husband or wife who bolsters the spouse's social and professional standing, or the partner whose family connections are useful in furthering a career. Of course, the same person may be both pleasant *and* useful, but either quality may stand without the other.

The third and highest good consists of that which is loved for its own sake, whether or not it is useful or pleasant. The things that we consider good may also bring us pleasure, but they also bring us at least as much pain and suffering. We might speak of the joy of playing football, running distance races, learning chemistry, writing a book, or raising children. But if we kept a log of the pleasurable and painful moments and made pleasure the basis for our decision, we would probably not do any of the above activities, nor much of anything else worthwhile.[46] If you perform any of these or similar activities, would you stop doing them if you calculated that the amount of pain outweighed the amount of pleasure? Probably not, or you would not be doing these difficult things in the first place. But we engage in these activities because we esteem them as good.[47] They give our life the wholeness, completeness, and balance that constitute the Roycean ideal and what we have been calling *teleological harmony.*

Friendship based on love of the good stands out as the highest possible kind of friendship. The person whom we love for his or her own sake will probably provide many happy moments. But like the arduous activities described in the previous paragraph, such friends might give us just as many or more moments of concern, sorrow, and even anger. But we love such persons because of the radiance of their being. In the philosophical tradition of Aristotle, especially as developed St. Thomas Aquinas, being is good, and evil is the privation of something that belongs to the nature of the thing.[48] We see good in men and women whose completeness and integrity exemplify the goodness of being.

Such goodness does not require perfection; if it did, there would be no real friendship. But the person who sees another as good, sees the wholeness beneath the flaws and sees the potential that unfolds as the person lives, works, and plays. We may understand such friendship better by comparing it to our admiration of people from afar. The person who shines for us as an exemplar of goodness might be a historical figure such as Washington, Lincoln, or Gandhi, or a recent cultural and spiritual leader such as Mother Teresa, Nelson Mandela, or Bono. But in these cases, the admiration goes in one direction. The people whom we admire are usually not arrogant, and they have an attitude of charity and philanthropic love for all of us; however, they cannot possibly know the vast majority of us. But when we see the good in someone whom we know personally and the recognition of good is mutual, we call it friendship.

Royce's view of friendship, or any personal relationship, stems from his distinction between descriptive and appreciative experience. Describable experiences are those that we can communicate publicly so that those who hear or read our descriptions know exactly what we mean. Much of our everyday knowledge such as prices, sizes, distances as well as all of our scientific knowledge can be described. Appreciative experience can be defined negatively as that which cannot be described publicly. These experiences include inner feelings that we might not be able to hold unchanged even in our own memory and cannot fully share with the public. To offer a simple example, we can describe the temperature of the water in a lake or pool by use of a thermometer. But if several people dive into the water, one may find it "shocking," another "refreshing," and still another "exhilarating." We may have a general idea of what each means but can never know exactly what they felt. If more people come to the pool, we can tell them the temperature of the water, but cannot know what they will feel, and each of them may have a different appreciative experience.

This brief digression on experience might convey the notion that descriptive experience refers to what is real and objective, while appreciate experience is limited to what is merely subjective. But to return to the main theme of experiencing friendship, we experience our friends appreciatively, and the friends and the friendships are real. We can describe our friends using any of the physical or social sciences such as the molecules that compose the human body, or the economic status of these individuals. But the aspect of the friend that is most important defies accurate description. Royce observes that a friend lives "in my daily world of experience" and poses the question, "In what sense is he real to me?" After showing that we cannot find our friend in scientific descriptions such as a field of molecules, he turns the focus to what is most important about the friend.

> His ideals which I so much admire, his will, which is so often much wiser than mine, his approval, which I prize so highly--where are all these?... Facts they are for me; and yet they are not facts *within* me nor yet are they describable facts in my space and in my time.[49]

Our friendship, like many of our appreciative relationships presupposes the reality of possibilities. For example, in writing a letter of recommendation a professor can *describe* a student's achievements as matters of fact: "This student had a 3.7 grade point average, was an officer in Student Government, and gave many hours of volunteer service." But we also estimate the student's capacities: "(he or she) will meet difficult academic challenges, get along well with a wide variety of people, work with discipline and focus." In these cases we are providing *appreciative* knowledge. These estimates can be wrong, of course, and people often fail to live up to their own potential. But the estimates provide indispensable guides for anyone making decisions, including admission committees and employers. Appreciative estimates of people constitute important thinking for many decision makers including athletic scouts, voters, and consumer of personal services. Royce uses the traditional philosophical terms "essence" or "nature" to denote a person's potential. He uses the example of a "potential poet." A young person who has not yet written a poem may or may not have the potential to write poems. But if he or she composes a poem, we reasonably estimate the potential for more poems. Likewise, when a city or hospital hires a person to be a firefighter or emergency room nurse, those making the hiring decision estimate that the one whom they hire has the potential to act courageously and lucidly in a life-threatening situation, even if he or she has not yet actually been in that situation.

In Royce's understanding of friendship, in fact of all human relations, we recognize in the other an expression of the universal mind of which we ourselves are fragments.[50] We estimate a friend as one who expresses and nourishes the teleological harmony that we have come to know and love as the ultimate good. We further see the other person, the friend or lover, as one who enables us to be saved from the curse of loneliness. In this beloved person, we get a glimpse of the universal beloved community that we can at least dimly see as the ultimate meaning of human existence. This love goes beyond Aristotle's categories of the merely pleasant or useful and provides a richer development of his notion of the good in itself.

Erotic Love

The term "love" most often applies to the special love that we can have for one person and involves sexual desire and erotic attraction as well as friendship. This discussion pertains to a heterosexual relationship but, changing what must be changed, it might also apply to a homosexual relationship. For most of us, this love is between a man and a woman. While we are young, we can often feel some sexual desire for many women or men, including those who could never be our friends much less marriage partners. But erotic love as a form of friendship goes well beyond sexual desire. Friendship means mutual recognition of good in the other, and if it is an erotic friendship, it involves also seeing beauty and mutual fulfillment embodied in the one we love. Love is not blind––it sees clearly the beauty that other people might miss. The term "erotic" has been badly used, but its original meaning stems from the Greek god Eros. Plato described the highest love as love of beauty itself and contended that love for a particular person is based on the beauty that he or she embodies.[51] As psychotherapist Rollo May explains, "Eros is the drive toward union with what we belong to––union with our own possibilities, union with significant other persons in our world in relation to whom we discover our own self-fulfillment." Contrasting Eros with sex, which involves pleasurable release, May continues, "But Eros is the mode of relating in which we do not seek release, but rather to cultivate, procreate, and form the world."[52] For May, erotic love, the desire to create meaning and beauty, constitutes the driving force behind the creation of what we have been calling "teleological harmony." [53]

A tragic aspect of life is that erotic love, sometimes called romantic love, often takes hold between two people who cannot sustain a long-term friendship necessary for marriage. Just as we may be sexually attracted to many people, we are capable of "falling in love" with many, although, usually not at the same time. When we fall in love, we feel that we have found our one-and-only; this love was "meant to be," "made in heaven." Psychiatrist Scott Peck describes falling in love as a dissolving of ego boundaries.[54] We meet a person to whom we are attracted and find we have so much in common that we melt together as one person. We re-enact Aristophanes' myth of finding our other half.

Psychologist Carl Jung interprets falling in love as projecting our ideal image of masculinity (*animus*) or femininity (*anima*) on a particular individual.[55] Of course, no man or woman could or should spend a lifetime playing out such a role. The overwhelming feeling of romantic love cannot last forever, and when it fades the all too human imperfections, which we previously overlooked or underestimated, now loom large. While erotic love clearly sees beauty, it might be blind to some other realities of the mortal man or woman clothed in the glow of light magnified by the desire of the lover. Hence the well-known saying, "the honeymoon's over." The challenge of a lasting love is learning to love this individual man or woman who exists independently of our personal dreams and ideals.

If we are fortunate, the person with whom we fall in love is also a person whose deepest wishes and desires we can admire and foster, and he or she reciprocates with admiration for us. Erotic love and friendship can join and become a lifetime enterprise. Friendship consists of enjoyment, gratitude, and enhancement of the good of the friend. Love that includes friendship is real love as opposed to mere "falling in love" or infatuation. While it hopefully includes erotic love, real love flows from a deeper part of the self and is more permanent. Scott Peck defines such love as "the willingness to extend yourself for the sake of spiritual growth in yourself and the one you love."[56] A very similar definition from Erich Fromm holds that love consists of "the active care for the growth of the one you love."[57] Both of these definitions make it clear that love consists not of feeling, but of *the habit of acting in a certain way.* The loving person develops habits or virtues of acting so that the good of the other person is enhanced. Even the most loving persons do not always *feel* like tending to the needs of their spouses or their children. But virtues are habits and habits take the form of a "second nature," developed over time by constant attention and repeated actions. Like the good musician, athlete, or medical professional, the loving person learns to make the right move "instinctively." That is why Erich Fromm called loving an *art.*

But like music, sports, and medical professions, loving is an art that must be learned. As Aristotle said of all virtues, they are not natural as instincts are, but we have the natural potential to learn them. So, we have to learn to love, and as with all learning, the most important aspect resides in practice. However, to practice correctly, to learn good habits, we need to know what to aim for. To achieve understanding most of us need at least an implied theory. Such a theory can be gleaned from examining what Royce described as the problem of individual life.

Love and the Problem of Life

Love is a problem because life is a problem.[58] In the following paragraphs I will develop the meaning of this statement. While reading this account, you may want to ask whether it coincides with your present outlook on life and love. The world as we find it does not seem right. We have a sense of uneasiness, a sense that things are not what they are supposed to be. Religions stand on this insight, that the world is lost, or fallen, and in need of redemption. Religions also offer a means of salvation.[59] Anti-religious cynics claim that religion deliberately creates the need for salvation the way an advertiser creates the need for a product. But the sense of wrongness goes deeper and creates the need for religion rather than religion creating the need. Perhaps no philosopher stated this discontent more powerfully than Plato who saw this world as a dark cave in which we mistake shadows for reality and which can be escaped through the practice of philosophy. That the awareness of something wrong is not limited to religious thinkers can be seen in the works of such atheist thinkers as Sigmund Freud, Karl Marx, and Ayn Rand. Each of them offered a way of salvation, namely, psychoanalysis, socialism, and capitalism, and each won a multitude of true believers. Whatever the cause of the human problem or the solution, we can begin with at least an acknowledgment that life is a problem.

Royce expressed the awareness of life's hardship very forcefully. He saw the emphasis in optimism that popular religion taught in his time. He stated: "...for all my idealism, I regret this popularity of optimism." [60] Royce contended that no one has "the right to the comfort that idealism offers" until they have known the tragedy of life and that "the misery of the finite world" is an essential part of the significance of the universe.[61] While Royce rejected the pessimism of materialism, he also rejected the kind of optimism that ignored the stubborn brutality of economic facts as well as the horrors in nature itself as revealed by Darwin.[62] Royce descends into the depth of pessimism in describing the challenges facing us. He contends that what most makes life sometimes appear as an evil dream is not the tragic heroism of standing up to clear enemy of the good. Rather, the bitterest experience of evil comes from the blind capriciousness of brute facts. We experience the problem of evil most cruelly:

> ...not because of conscious sinfulness...but because mere brute accident or stupidity tears to pieces whatever is spiritual, kills our infant children, leaves our unrecognized heroes to die neglected and ineffective, sunders the wounded hearts of faithful lovers, makes brother war with brother, plunges society into bitter confusion, defeats over and over our most sacred ideals. [63]

Royce does not find the way out of pessimism through an easy optimism that treats the suffering of this world as relatively insignificant. Rather, he cites the symbolism of Christianity, which depicts the Creator Spirit, the *Logos,* [64] not as an aloof Pure Spirit, but as one who bodily becomes one of us, suffers with us, dies, and descends into hell. Royce believed in the ultimate victory of the Creative Spirit, which means teleological harmony, but this triumph does not come *without the most strenuous action on the part of each of us.* Such is the problem of life.

A loving friendship does not offer a solution to the problem of human life, but it offers a glimpse of what a solution would be. Josiah Royce offers friendship as one of the "sources of religious insight." His description is worth quoting.

> For human society as it now is, in this world of care, is a chaos of needs; and the whole social order groans and travails together in pain until now, longing for salvation. It can be saved, only in case there is some way that leads upward, through all turmoil and social bickering, to a realm where that vision of unity and self-possession which our clearest moments bring to us becomes not merely vision, but

fulfillment, where love finds its own, and where the power of the spirit triumphs.[65]

Friendship and love give us an insight into what human society can be when the chaos of individual needs is brought into harmony. Friends and lovers do not just think about or imagine such a harmony; they experience it as a reality.

The social experience of harmony and overcoming of egoistic boundaries may occur not only on the level of two persons, but on the level of groups and whole societies. A person may have a love greater than self for a religious community, a sports team, a military unit, a group of professional associates, or even a nation. These experiences give a glimpse of what universal harmony can be, but they have obvious limits. The group is in discord in relation to other groups. Discord stands out most tragically in a military unit, whose role puts them in mortal combat with other groups, but discord among groups also persists in any competitive exclusivity, or zero-sum games in which the victory of each side comes at the expense of competitors. This kind of exclusivity occurs most conspicuously in politics, business, and sports, but may also take place in science, art, religion or any other human activity.

Further, the harmony that a person has for a group, or that two people have for each other, has moments of intense disharmony and may break apart altogether and the "chaos of needs" returns. Nevertheless, the experience of harmony gives us clear first-hand knowledge of the good toward whose realization we can devote our best efforts.

Awareness of the full reality of relationship can create a *reverence for all the relationships of life*. As Frank Oppenheim elaborates on Royce's insight, reverence for the relations of life can occur when:

...authentic union is felt in a family, or between true friends, or in authentic educational experiences, in deep interpersonal communications, in the genuine mutual trust of compacting business partners as together they face a risky future, in a scientific group's authentic searching for further findings, and in an artist's creative in-touch-ness with his or her inmost genius.[66]

The reverence that we learn personally can guide us in our attitude toward all relations. The person who reveres relations will abstain from recklessness, arrogance, and any other attitude that leads to destructive behavior. A community can be *genuine* in Royce's sense only if it is based on loyalty to loyalty, which respects the diversity of loyal causes. The reverent person will see all relations, not just his or her own, as contributing to the genuine universal community. Our loving relationships serve as our best teachers of ethical behavior.

What is Desirable as Opposed to Merely Desired?

To further analyze problems that emerge in the area of love and friendship, we use the question posed at the end of the first chapter and the beginning of this chapter. For example, how can we distinguish the desirable from the merely desired in our relations involving sex? The view toward sex that dominates our popular culture, expressed in such things as TV sitcoms and movies, can be called "social libertarianism." The term "social libertarian" as used here refers to those who believe that every person should have the maximum amount of freedom compatible with the freedom of others. The libertarians argue that there should be neither laws nor social pressures to prohibit anyone from doing whatever they want to do as long as it does not harm or deliberately deceive anyone else. Some social libertarians argue that sex has no more importance than any other social interaction and the only moral bounds are the avoidance of force and fraud. Social libertarians have no problem with casual sex of any kind as long as it is between "consenting adults." [67] This view has credence among some ethicists who embrace the libertarian view. Such thinkers sometimes compare sex to an encounter between a shopper and a clerk or between two tennis players. They might say, "I have a regular tennis partner, but I may play with anyone who wants to play." I once heard an instructor in a counselor-education program likewise dismiss the notion that sex is something sacred and profound. He said, "Sex is fun, but so is riding my bicycle." He must have had an underdeveloped attitude toward sex. Either that or he really liked that bike.

For most of us sex is a powerful force with great potential for good or for harm. The ethical question in this section asks whether, after thoughtful deliberation, an action may be considered desirable, and not merely *desired*. Plato describes desire as a many-headed monster that each of us has within us, and which can overwhelm and replace our very humanity. Desires kept under the control of reason are good as, for instance, the desire for food can lead to nourishment and the desire for sex can lead to couple-bonding and children. We desire pleasure, and pleasure is good. A hedonistic slogan of many young people in the 1960s was "If it feels good, do it." But desires that run out-of-control lead to displeasure and disintegration. A life of pleasure seeking and yielding to all of our desires does not add up to a pleasant life, much less a good life. Eating the foods that taste the best in the quantities that we desire can lead to catastrophic health problems. Tobacco, binge drinking of alcohol, drugs, and excessive sunbathing can all feel pleasurable in the short-run, and so they are desired. Promiscuous sex has a prominent place on this list. But the ethical question in each case asks whether these activities are *desirable*. Do we desire them when we understand their full and long-term implications?

Sexual desire exemplifies the desire for personal pleasures mentioned above; what is *desired* as pleasurable is not necessarily *desirable*. Most young men and women rate many women and men desirable; a natural physical attraction makes itself strongly felt. But sex with every person whom we find attractive would not be desirable if we understood all of the implications. The obvious problems are pregnancies for couples who are not ready to raise a child, or who are not even couples in any real sense, and the danger of sexually transmitted disease. But even if "safe sex" avoids pregnancy and disease, promiscuous sex can cause enormous personal suffering. Men and women often have a hard time understanding each other in the best of circumstances, and in a short-term relationship, one or the other might mistake a casual encounter for a loving commitment. A relationship that turns out to be illusory or fraudulent often leads to deep hurt and sometimes to violent behavior. *The reason is that sex involves such a deep commitment of body, emotions, and sense of self.* The *desirability* of sex depends on the long-range effects on each person, actual and possible offspring, and third parties to whom either person has a commitment. The argument of this chapter, contrary to the libertarian argument, is that sex, like all desired activities, can be desirable or not depending on thoughtful considerations of its context and long-range implications.

These considerations lead to our second general question: *How can you best enhance your personal integrity as well as that of other persons and your integration with each other?* Desirable conduct in love and friendship is that which enhances integrity and integration as components of *teleological harmony.* If the analysis presented here so far is correct, there are certain sexual acts that are clearly wrong. These include rape, sexual contact with a child, sex with the possible transmission of disease, and sex based on lies or false promises. Even the social libertarians consider these wrong because of the almost inevitable great harm as well as violating the moral prohibition against merely using another person. But sometimes sex, even between consenting adults, especially when taken thoughtlessly, can leave lives in ruins. The observations presented here can provide a strong incentive for commitment to a long term and mutually understood commitment of two people to each other. Most people express this commitment through marriage.[68] Of course marriages also can be good or bad, and sometimes can even be as casual and thoughtless as unmarried sex. But if two people take monogamy seriously, they will know and love each other, commit themselves to their mutual long-range happiness, and develop the ability to care for children in a two-parent home.[69] Like any human activity, marriage deserves to be called "good" if and only if it contributes to teleological harmony. Abuse, dominance, neglect, and infidelity destroy families. An attitude of mutual love and respect, which leads to the growth of each member of the family, constitutes the prototype of ethical living.

How Moral Imagination Nourishes the Good in Relationships

We can apply moral imagination to any relationship that we have or will have: parents, brothers and sisters, friends, boyfriends or girlfriends, roommates, professors, administrators, bosses, employees, spouses, children. Moral imagination requires *vision* of what you can be if you actualize your potential—realize your *telos*. How would you treat the people in your life if you were the best person that you can be? This question is not meant to conjure up an unrealistic notion of an ideal person, but the person that you can realistically be, based on your own background, temperament, and talent.

Further, you can envision what the other persons would be if they realized their own potential. This does not mean imposing your values on them, but rather seeing where *their* unique path can lead. This is difficult, but anytime that you can see a person's potential and communicate faith that you have in them, you help them to become their best self. You may have had parents, teachers, coaches, or others who have done this for you. Seeing potential leads to growth and flourishing; failure to see potential leads to stagnation and decay.

Ella Lyman Cabot, student and friend of Royce, defined imagination, meaning moral imagination, as "...the ability to see others as they see themselves." She adds, "Imagination trains the power to see other people's joys and sorrows as though they were our own."[70] Cabot contends that brutal acts follow from lack of imagination. Many hurtful actions are not the result of deliberate bad-will, but of what Royce called, "deliberate inattention." Cabot advises that we can train our imagination by deliberately looking at other people with the awareness that their inner joys and sorrow have the same intensity to them, as ours do to us. As Cabot states it:

> Because imagination gives the power to see others as they see themselves, it is one of the sustaining qualities in friendship. Friends can rest in the loyalty of the person of quick and trained sympathy. [71]

To live ethically entails that we strive to develop moral imagination toward everyone whom we come across, but especially to those who would be our friends and lovers.

Developing and applying moral imagination is seldom easy. Remaining inert and dwelling in the past with its resentments takes less effort. The word "resentment" comes from the Latin *re-sentiment,* which means to feel the same things over and over. Such an attitude leads to autointoxication or self-poisoning, blocking off the ability to appreciate the inner life of other people, friends as well as strangers. Wallowing in resentment is easier than striving to develop imagination, but the easiest path does not mean the best path. Making the effort to develop moral imagination leads to happiness and teleological harmony.

CHAPTER 5
Business Ethics

The Ethical Dimension of Business Decisions

Business ethics does not consist of a separate set of values and purposes apart from those we use in dealing with friends and family. Rather, business ethics means the study of moral goods as applied to business practices and decisions. This chapter will argue that the good, as *teleological harmony,* should constitute the goal of every ethical decision in business. As stated in Chapter 1, Royce's concept of teleological harmony can be understood as purposive integration. Ethical decisions reflect and enhance the personal integrity of the business decision maker as well as the integration of those factors of society that produce, distribute, and consume the economic goods of that society.

The following discussion pertains specifically to those who work, or will work, in for-profit business. However, most of the insights can be applied to every sector of work including such not-for-profit areas as health care, education, government, religion, and philanthropy. As you read the following paragraphs, ask whether they offer insights that can guide you in your current or future employment.

In addition to teleological harmony, the Roycean concept of "reverence for relations" serves as a guide for ethical decision making. Every business decision directly involves relations. For a private owner the primary relations are with customers and suppliers. For those working in companies that they do not own, there is a large and diverse array of relations between the company and the employee as well as a complex network of relations among co-workers, superiors, and subordinates. In all cases there are relationships with customers and with the local communities as well as with the larger society.

Every business decision has an ethical dimension. The ethical aspect of every business decision resides in the fact that business decisions create or destroy wealth on which people depend to achieve all of their goods in life from food to education. In addition to affecting wealth, business decisions affect the well-being of people in many aspects of their lives. Most obviously, the people with whom we work are directly affected by our decisions. Business decisions can also affect a wide range of other "stakeholders." These include employees, investors and creditors, customers, suppliers, competitors, taxpayers, and, in some cases, everyone who lives in the environment of our business.

Ethical behavior on the part of those in business requires that they are aware of possible wide-ranging and long-term effects of their decisions. Therefore, they must avoid what Robert Solomon calls "moral myopia" and "tunnel vision."[72] To understand what may be considered *desirable,* we need a clear understanding of the purpose of business. The purpose might not match up exactly with what motivates individuals to start a business or work for a business. The individual's motive might be to simply make a living or to strike it rich. These personal goals may be the purpose in the sense of answering the question, "Why are you doing this?" But for persons to act ethically they need to understand how their work fits into the larger scheme of things. A person who looks only at the next monthly receipts or paycheck is likely to overlook both the opportunities for doing good and the dangers of allowing or even contributing to harm.

The Purpose of Business

Some argue that the purpose of business is simply to make a profit. Those who hold this position assert that persons who manage companies that they do not own have only one duty, to maximize profit for the owners. If they manage a public corporation, their only duty is to the shareholders; there are no other stakeholders. The advocates of profit-making as the goal of business rightly assess profit as a good thing affirming that managers have a fiduciary obligation to increase the wealth of the owners or shareholders. The problem arises when managers see profit as the *only* good and the shareholders as the *only* stakeholders.

The major theme of this book highlights the truth that human actions are purposeful and that we can identify the good of anything we do by looking closely at the purpose of the action. The previous paragraph referred to profit-making as good, but also alluded to ethical problems that arise from making profit the *exclusive* good. The key to understanding ethical profit-making lies in knowing the *purpose* of profit. Some might argue that the reason managers and owners strive for profit is to make themselves rich, and therefore that constitutes their purpose. When people think this way, there is little that can prevent them from slipping into practices that are bad business as well as bad ethics. The single-minded practice of seeking profit without producing real wealth in the form of goods and services has led to catastrophic results in recent times. One of the early notorious cases involved the executives of Enron who, intent on showing a profit, lost sight of their responsibility to run an energy company. Their moral blindness destroyed the wealth of thousands of employees, pensioners, and investors. The whole series of "bubbles" from high-tech stocks to real estate were created by avaricious speculation.

Royce held that much evil results from deliberate inattention rather than the deliberate will to do evil. We are responsible for the foreseeable outcomes of our actions, even if we do not make the effort to actually foresee them. The example of the Enron executives was one example. We can also look at wider, more global examples. Michael Lewis, analyzing the world-wide financial crisis of the twenty-first century provides a glaring example of how the financial sector, looking only at increasing profits, instead of at the real economy, led to disaster for the whole economic system. Lewis sums it up: "What appeared to be economic growth was activity fueled by people borrowing money they probably couldn't afford to repay."[73] Lewis cites Iceland as a microcosm of the debt-fueled illusory increase in wealth. Between 2003, when Iceland de-regulated the financial industry and privatized the banks, to 2007, the price of Icelandic real estate tripled, and stocks increased nine-fold. The little that Icelanders knew about investment banking came from young Icelanders who had studied in American business schools. Lewis infers that the problems of Iceland showed as much about the "American soul" as about the Icelanders. As Lewis describes the Icelandic bankers:

> They understood instantly, for instance, that finance has less to do with productive enterprise than trading bits of paper among themselves. And when they lent money, they didn't simply facilitate enterprise but bankrolled friends and family so that they might buy and own things, like real investment bankers.

> That was the biggest American financial lesson the Icelanders took to heart the importance of buying as many assets as possible with borrowed money, as asset prices only rose.[74]

As some economist predicted, and all of them should have seen, the price of assets also falls. The collapse of Iceland's illusory prosperity prefigured the collapse of the world-wide economy. The single-minded grasping for profit without concern for real wealth stems from a lack of integrity in the form of deliberate inattention and leads to economic disintegration.

Classical capitalists such as Andrew Carnegie, John D. Rockefeller, and J. P. Morgan created epic fortunes, eclipsed by more recent entrepreneurs such as Bill Gates and Warren Buffet. There are many others, but of the ones I mentioned, none pursued profit with tunnel vision; rather they responsibly took care of businesses that created wealth for millions of others and for the nation as a whole. We find the ethical purpose of profit not by an assessment of what motivates this or that person in business; we find the purpose of profit by looking at its role in the grand network of relations that make up what we call business.

"Profit" received a bad name early in western civilization. Aristotle, and nearly a millennium later, St. Thomas Aquinas, held that products had a "natural" value based on the labor that produced them. Any profit over and above the fair payment of the worker constituted theft. A contemporary example to support the traditional scorn of profit-takers can be found in the ticket scalper at sporting events. The scalper buys the tickets from the ticket office at a price affordable to many fans. He (nearly all of them are men) then sells it at a higher price and pockets the difference. The profit made by the scalper adds no value to the ticket. The notion that a profit-taker does not add anything to the product is found in the term "robber baron," a term frequently applied to the founders of industrial capitalism.

The term "robber baron" originates from stories, true or not, about medieval barons who would tax traffic along the Rhine for the right to pass safely by their castles.[75] The barons contributed no value to the product and their "profit" was simply theft. The pioneers of American industry at times used their economic and political clout in ways that reminded writers of the robber barons, but while these industrialists were not always exemplars of virtue, they nevertheless created real wealth. They were capitalists in the proper sense of the word, in that they put up the "capital," the seed money, which purchased the equipment, machinery, railroads, and all the technology that provided for a modern industrialized economy. Although often antagonistic toward each other, capitalists and workers together produced the wealth that we enjoy today.

The Ethical Meaning of Profit

Profit constitutes a means to the *real purpose* of business, which is providing goods and services. The purpose of profit is to make capital available, and capital is needed for the maintenance, improvement, and expansion of business. Peter Drucker offered the analogy of profits to breathing. An organism needs to breathe in order to live. But breathing does not constitute the purpose of life. So, while profit is necessary for the life of a business, the profit ought to serve the business; the business does not exist for the profit.

Profit making has other positive meanings. For one, it is the indicator of success in the market. It shows that the business is producing what consumers want at a price they are willing to pay. The profitable business produces more wealth than it is uses up. Further, profit rewards the risk of the persons or institutions who put up the capital to make the business possible. It follows that management has an ethical duty to enhance the wealth of owners and investors if the latter are share*olders*. If the above analysis of the ethical meaning of profit is correct, it follows that management has no duty to stock speculators and "day traders." During the decade of the 1990s when stocks were steadily climbing, a private investor could buy stocks in the morning and sell them in the evening at a profit. It was easy for almost anyone to imagine him or herself to be a financial genius. As in any gambling adventure, players could gain personal wealth if they quit while they were ahead. But they contributed no real wealth to the economy.

Creating wealth for owners and shareholders constitutes one of the duties of those who manage businesses. Their other duties include producing goods and services that improve the lives of customers. Ethical management entails that the products be of high quality and that they do not impose unnecessary or unknown danger to the consumer. Further, it means that managers treat all employees fairly and with dignity, that they enact reasonable procedures to protect the physical environment, and that they treat all suppliers and competitors fairly.

The Ethical Duty of Management

Many of the ethical duties of management are prescribed by law. These areas include worker safety, fair labor practices, anti-discrimination, anti-harassment, environmental protection, fair trade practices, truth in advertising and packaging, and financial disclosure. The law expresses the minimum standard of society's ethical values. A basic duty in business is to obey the law. So, the first question that a person making a management decision should ask is, "Is it legal?" Laws are made by human legislators and are not perfect. However, laws give us a common standard to follow. Further, violation of the law can cause career-shattering problems for individuals and financial disasters for companies. There may be emergencies in which a technical violation of the law is necessary to avoid further harm, but these are rare. One such example was related to the author by a mid-level manager of an industrial corporation who was in charge of a company water treatment facility. A pump failed and the rising water threatened expensive and essential equipment. There was no time for consultation and so he chose to release the untreated water into the river until the pump could be repaired. He immediately reported the mishap to the plant manager who sent the facts to the company environmental department who in turn informed the E. P. A. Environmental and legal damages were held to a minimum and the manager who made the decision was not reprimanded.[76] A person who violates a law in such a situation must be prepared to justify his or her decision in a public forum, and, if necessary, in a court of law. Aside from rare examples, an ethical manager obeys the law.

But although legality stands out as a necessary criterion for ethical decisions, mere legality is not sufficient. Ethical standards hold true whether or not there is a specific law to enforce them. We have the duty to avoid harm, deceit, unfairness, and disrespect, whether such acts would cause legal problems or not. Furthermore, even in areas regulated by law, management may have information or insights based on experience that exceed the scope of the law. They might test their decisions by asking, whether they would want people whom they love to use this product, live in this environment, or work under these conditions. This thought experiment might require "moral imagination." "If I had a son or daughter working in this industry..." Or, "If I were a poor person living in a developing country..." These considerations help us to know what is *desirable* and therefore good business practice.

Personal Integrity and Management

In the introductory chapter, the second question offered as a way to think about ethical questions asked, "How can you best enhance your personal integrity as well as that of other persons and your integration with each other?" Personal integrity provides the foundation for institutional integrity. Further, personal integrity is the area for which each individual can take control and responsibility. Integrity and integration stem from the Latin work *integer,* meaning "whole." We can best understand integrity by seeing it not so much as an adjective, a static quality, that some people have and others lack. Rather, we do better to think of integrity as a verb. Life is dynamic, always changing, and from early childhood on, we are integrating or disintegrating.

Integrity shows most clearly in the virtues of honesty and truthfulness; these qualities are often used as synonyms for integrity. Disintegrating persons do not connect what they believe with what they say. Therefore, their words are not always truthful and never trustworthy. Or their actions do not connect with their own moral values. For instance, a person might profess the ideals of Christianity or Judaism on the weekends, but act during the workweek in ways that are inconsistent with what they believe. Moral blindness may shelter them from any sense of wrongdoing.

Further cases of disintegration show up in those who maintain that selfishness is a virtue and that our only moral guide is to "look out for number one." Such persons fail to integrate their own good with the good of the overlapping communities and the general society on which their own good depends. They maintain that their wealth belongs solely to them because they created all of it with their own labor, and they maintain that philanthropy is not a duty and that all taxation is a form of theft. Those who hold this view believe that they have no duty to other people except "negative duties." They grant that we must avoid directly harming or cheating another person, but we have no duty for example, to prevent people from starving, or dying of disease. Those who adhere to the thinking of Ayn Rand exemplify this attitude and identify their brand of self-centered individualism with "capitalism." It is interesting to draw the contrast between these ideological capitalists and real capitalists such as Warren Buffet who, on the occasion of giving away a large portion of his fortune, credited Andrew Carnegie with the statement that "huge fortunes that flow in large part from society should in large part be returned to society."[77]

In addition to the persons who forget their ideals when in a business setting, or those whose ideals are disconnected to the society of which they constitute a part, another disintegrating type consists of people who *have no* consistent ideals. Business ethicist Robert Solomon described business students in the 1980s, who believed that they needed and deserved an annual income of $75,000 to $100,000 (in 1989 dollars) just to live. The 1980s constituted a period when the "Greed is good" idolatry was at its peak.[78] Solomon describes these students in their thoughts about their business careers:

There was very little thought or speculation about the social relations that actually define most business communities. Little thought about what they would actually do to *earn* the money they made, and virtually no thought whatever (for most of them) about what product or service the company they would work for would actually produce."[79]

Students with integrity would strive to learn how to best work within an organization and how their skills would enhance their company and contribute to the larger society.

Royce scholar, Griffin Trotter, in his 1997 book, *The Loyal Physician,* compares the narrow concern for profit with the "winning is everything" attitude in sports. Playing sports can teach young people the value of discipline, teamwork, fair play, and how skills are learned by patient and dedicated practice. Of course, athletes play to win; that is one of the ways in which the lessons of sports are learned. But winning has little if any value if it comes at the expense of the more important character traits that sports can teach. Trotter quotes Royce on the matter of education through sports:

Fair play in sports is a peculiarly good instance of loyalty. And in insisting upon the spirit of fair play, the elders who organize our youthful sports can do a great work for the nation. The coach, or other leader in sports, to whom fair play is not a first concern is, simply, a traitor to our youth and to our nation.[80]

Royce's idea of the loyal coach applies, by analogy, to the loyal person of business whose priority consist in producing goods and services that enhance human flourishing. Trotter, who is a physician, places his critique of business ethics in the context of the economic aspect of health care. He concludes that since the Roycean model is not widely accepted in business, health care professionals must take care to avoid the business attitude that puts the bottom line above other considerations. Physicians and other health care professionals can be and should be well compensated, without losing sight of loyalty to the ideals of their professions.[81] We can draw the further conclusion that the task of anyone trying to teach or practice business ethics consists of developing integrity that puts loyalty to higher ideals, producing goods and services that enhance human flourishing, above the narrow goal of accumulating money.

Nourishing Integrity in the Workplace

Royce had argued that it takes time and much social interaction for each of us humans to become moral persons with the ability to choose right and wrong. As explained in Chapter Two, we begin life, not as a unified self, but as a cluster of conflicting aims passions and desires. We achieve a unified self by developing a plan by which we live our lives. We learn the possible life plans through imitation. We begin our moral and social development in infancy and it continues as we learn, through imitation, to speak, eat, dress, play, work, and interact in countless ways with others. Royce does not say that we choose our life plan from a menu, but that the example of other people suggests life plans enabling each of us to choose our own unique plan.[82] Royce offers *loyalty to loyalty* as the criterion for distinguishing good from bad life plans. This ideal may be interpreted in more familiar language as universal respect for all persons.

Royce's analysis of moral development pertains to our contemporary business settings. Each person consists of multiple and conflicting social roles, plans and desires. For example, an employee must interact with superiors, colleagues, subordinates, customers, vendors, as well as with those who enforce laws and regulations. Moreover, young people coming into the business world probably desire, security, wealth, reputation, the pride and prestige of excelling in their work, and a desire to fulfill their notion of what it means to be "a good person." These conflicting forces may lead to a loss of personal integrity as well as disharmony among individuals. Contemporary business ethics must deal with this universal human challenge of building integrity. The task of the business leader is to first of all exhibit personal integrity.

Besides exhibiting personal integrity, the task of the ethical business leader is to develop integrity within the workplace. The challenge of creating an ethical workplace includes the recognition that the workplace itself must consciously and deliberately foster the development of integrity. The manager cannot assume that all employees govern their own behavior by a consistent "moral compass." As stated by Royce and by contemporary business ethicists, most people have several "ethical selves"[83] A person may be decent, honest, and respectful with friends and family, but deceitful, arrogant, and greed-driven at work. Lawrence Kohlberg's study of moral development shows that even adults may operate, at least in some area of their lives, at a "conventional level," associated with late childhood and early teenage. At this level, called social concordance, the person acts according to his or her perception of group expectations. So, if a person comes into a workplace with the assumption that business is about making a profit by doing whatever it takes, that assumption will drive the person's behavior.

Using the metaphor of "bad apples," ethicists Linda Trevino and Katherine Nelson contend that much bad behavior results from "bad barrels," corporate cultures that fail to promote ethical behavior. Addressing senior managers who are supportive of creating an ethical culture, the authors write: "Then, it is up to you to contribute to the larger organizational culture by creating a work environment that supports ethical conduct and integrity for the people you manage."[84] Integrity, meaning wholeness, means bringing the multiple ethical selves together, so that the behavior in the workplace matches the behavior of the person at his or her best. Managers create such an atmosphere by good example, by making ethical standards clear, by reinforcing the standards with constant reminders, and by implementing clear and consistent rewards and punishments.

The most fundamental principle of ethical behavior consists of treating every person with respect. This would mean minimally that a person would avoid doing anything to harm another, humiliating anyone, or doing anything to make the workplace unnecessarily stressful and hostile. A basic attitude of respect entails looking out for worker safety and avoidance of discrimination and sexual harassment, or any form of harassment.

Beyond avoiding harm, respect for co-workers entails positively supporting their efforts to become better workers and better persons. This can take the form of encouraging, teaching, mentoring and being generally supportive. Integration means seeing the workplace as a community, meaning that it involves a network of shared relationships as well as shared values, goals, and meanings. In his book on *Heroic Leadership*, Chris Lowney, a former Jesuit, and international managing director for J. P. Morgan, describes the qualities of leadership that apply equally to religious orders, corporations, schools, football teams, and families. He sums up one of these principles:

> Love-driven leaders hunger to see latent potential blossom and to help it happen. In more prosaic terms, when do children, students, athletes, or employees achieve their full potential? When they are parented, taught, coached, or managed by those who engender trust, provide support and encouragement, uncover potential, and set high standards.[85]

Lowney's observation corresponds to the Roycean notions of imagination and awareness of potential that were discussed in Chapter 3.

In an atmosphere of mutual respect, loyalty, and love, each person enables his or her co-workers, superiors and subordinates to bring out their best in work and in life. A sign of such community manifests itself in the workers referring to the company, or at least their part of it as "we" rather than "they" or "it". Workers, from the executive level on down, are better persons and better workers when they can identify the good of the company with their own good. Of course, this statement holds true only if the identity is based on reality and not on illusion. The executives of Enron were encouraging their employees to invest their retirement savings in Enron while the executives were dumping their own Enron stock. By contrast, companies in which every employee from the CEO to the hourly wage earners treat each other respectfully and have reverence for their relationship are more likely to thrive ethically and economically.

Reverence for Relations

Problems that provide ethical opportunities and dangers involve three kinds of relations: the relations among the members of the firm; the relations between the individual and the firm; and the relations between the firm and the larger society. In each case, ethical behavior flows from reverence for these relations; bad behavior oozes from neglect and disrespect for the relations.[86] The well-being of each individual as well as for the organization itself depends on the health of the relations.

Within any working environment, such as a mill, an office, a hospital, or construction project, each person has the ethical duty to respect his or her co-workers, superiors, and subordinates. An attitude of respect excludes any form of harassment, discrimination, deception, or ill-temper that creates a hostile environment and hurts the person as well as the work. Those who have a respect for themselves and for other human beings and a reverence for their relations create an environment of support and encouragement in which all individuals can flourish as persons and as workers.

Workers owe their employers honest work for their pay. Every worker, including those at the executive level, must avoid conflicts of interest. Such conflicts are situations in which the employee could gain at the expense of the employer. Examples include an employee with purchasing responsibility who has ownership in a supplier, or any person with decision making power who is invested in a competitor. Purchasers should also avoid "gifts" from vendors that could be construed as bribes. Also, such things as trade secrets must be respected. In summary, employees should know and honor the company's code of ethics.

The companies, in the persons of those who make and enforce policy, owe to the workers in addition to their pay, a workplace free of unnecessary hazards, pollutants, harassment, and the psychological pollution of bad bosses. Honesty and respect stand out as indispensable for an ethical workplace. Ethics in the workplace requires that the men and women at the highest levels practice, communicate, and require ethical behavior at every level.

In citing the duties of the company to the larger society, we can sum up the essential characteristics of the ethical business leader. All ethical actions require an ever-expanding awareness of who is affected by our actions and how they are affected. While profits are necessary for business, they are not the sole purpose, nor the sole duty of business leadership. The ethical duties of the business leader include providing products and services that improve the life of consumers and others who are affected by the products. Acting ethically in business also includes respecting the law, treating all persons fairly, creating a healthy work place and caring for the natural environment. Ethical leadership requires integrity, which means integrating our words and actions with our ideals, integrating our personal good with that of our company, and integrating our company's good with that of the larger society in which we live and work.

The duties of the company to the larger society require that the companies obey the law and avoid all unnecessary harm to their customers and the environment. Companies, as well as individuals, need to avoid moral myopia and tunnel vision. What companies do impact the whole economy, especially the local economy in which they work. Ethical leadership requires moral imagination to bring about the least amount of harm and the greatest teleological harmony possible.

So, in your work-life, how can you enhance your own good and the common good? I have argued that you begin by being aware of how every decision, large and small, stands as an opportunity to enhance your personal integrity and to make the workplace an atmosphere for you and others to flourish. Each decision also poses the danger of disintegration. Moving in a good direction entails focusing on the true purpose of your work, which involves more than company profit and your personal paycheck. It involves respect for individuals and reverence for the relations both within your organization and with the larger community. These goals are enhanced by thoughtful study of the real circumstances of your situation so that you can discern what is truly desirable, and the use of moral imagination to bring about the greatest good, which consists of purposive integration.

CHAPTER 6
Living Ethically in a Consumerist Society

The Problem of Abundance

In looking at the features that characterize the United States in the early part of the twenty-first century, nothing stands out more than the abundance of material goods that we consume. Whether we judge this as a compliment to our economic success or an indictment of our spiritual and cultural shallowness, the fact remains that we consume prodigiously, and most of us enjoy the abundance and would not have it otherwise. Given the reality that we are consumers in a consumerist society, how do we approach this reality ethically? I will try to show that the same ethical guidelines that apply to aspects of life, such as friendship and business ethics, apply also to the consumption of products. We need to distinguish the *merely desired* from the *desirable* and to find ways to create *teleological harmony* through personal and social integration. We will look first at the ethical duty of the consumer as it affects ourselves and others. Next, we can carry the ethical process to the next level by integrating our human culture with a healthy natural environment. We will consider the consumerist society in the context of the larger picture of the environment, followed by some suggestions as to what kind of public policy an ethical person might promote.

The Ethical Duty of Consumers

The ethical duty of the consumer rests on the fact that when we make a purchase, we vote for that product. Our dollars constitute votes, and the things on which most of us spend our dollars are the things that producers will manufacture and sell. In a market economy, business decision-makers, large and small, try to anticipate what we will buy and how much we are willing to pay. If they judge correctly, we buy the products that they produce and their business thrives. While our motive for buying a product consists primarily of our wanting it, our purchases also affect our natural and cultural environment by rewarding the decision to produce and sell the product and thereby motivating the company as well as its competitors to produce more. So, if we collectively buy, for example, a lot of SUVs, garden supplies, tennis rackets, and diet colas, a lot of these items will be on the market; if we quit buying them, they would disappear. The purchasers of each of these products presumably judge them as economic *goods*.

The study of ethics calls for us to ask in what sense purchased items are good. While it seems that a single purchase does not make an appreciable difference, we have an ethical duty to treat our purchases as important. We can draw a parallel with political voting. Very rarely does an election come down to one vote, and so it would seem that if you stay home on Election Day nothing changes. A character in B. F Skinner's novel, *Walden II,* observed that in a national election, there is a greater chance that you will be in an automobile accident on your way to the polling place than there is that your vote will make a difference. But if we take the election process seriously, we go to vote, trusting that enough other people who share our values will do the same, and collectively we make a difference. It might seem that an election is a "zero sum game," one candidate wins and the other loses. For each candidate, it is "all or nothing." But if we look more closely, we realize that if our candidates win, we might prefer a landslide so that the office holders of our choice will have a mandate to enact the legislation or programs that we voted for. If our candidates loses, we prefer a close election so that the winning candidate will be forced to respect the minority positions on issues. So, in a sense, every vote does count. Likewise, in voting with our purchases, we, and those who think like us, make a difference. But in the market place even more so than in the polling place, every "vote" counts; every purchase rewards the seller. Therefore, we need to ask whether what we *desire* is really *desirable*.

In an economic sense, spending is good, since every dollar that we spend becomes someone else's income. But like most good things, more is not necessarily better. Failure to save a portion of our income leads to serious problems both for the individual and the society. We generally promote good by spending in moderation. However, our specific spending has a good or bad impact on ourselves and on the producer. For example, if we buy locally grown fresh fruits and vegetables, we obtain nutritious food and support local growers. By contrast, if we buy pornographic material, we need to question the impact on ourselves and ask what kind of industry we are supporting. Even in industries that produce good products, a full ethical analysis must take account of the conditions of the labor that produces them, whether the labor consists of immigrant farm workers or "sweat shops" in developing countries.

In making any purchase, we should first ask how the product or service will affect us as human beings who are mortal, social, rational, free, creative, and have the potential to be something more. A good purchase enhances our growth in at least one of these dimensions and does not detract significantly from any of them. We can easily make a list of purchases that do this, from food to athletic equipment, from books to musical instruments and hobby supplies. The question may come up as to whether we can really call this an issue. Why would people buy products that they did not think will enhance their lives? Several reasons stand out, especially addiction. People succumb to obvious culprits, such as drugs, alcohol, tobacco, and gambling. Other items for purchase, which may or may not be addictions in a clinical sense, entail irrational consumption and futile attempts to meet some acquired need. For example, while food is one of our most important goods, more and more people are succumbing to overeating, making obesity a national health crisis. Others have a need to shop and buy things whether they need them or not. And people who buy things as a means of social competition need to ask themselves if the purchase really enhances their life. Consumption as a kind of competition seems to be fiercest among adolescents, but some people never outgrow it. In the years leading up to the recession of 2007, many people bought homes by taking out loans that they could not repay. This over-reaching led to extreme hardship both for the individual borrower and for the whole economy.

In addition to asking about the impact of our purchase on us, we need to ask about its impact on those around us when we use the product, and we need to be aware of the conditions necessary for the availability of the product. For instance, while we cannot eat meat without killing animals, how much unnecessary animal suffering are we willing to permit? Is our desire for cheap oil worth our entanglements in the Middle East? Would we pay more for electricity in order to reduce greenhouse gasses or to improve the safety of miners and coal haulers?

Consumption and the Ethics of the Enlightenment

We can best enhance our thinking about consumption and the environment by doing what truly educated people do, look at the larger picture. The modern age is a time of secularization and loss of the *sacred*. We could describe the *sacred* or *holy* as that which deserves *reverence*.

> Chapter 3 on love and friendship referred to Frank Oppenheim's observation that reverence for relations constitutes a necessary condition for full appreciation of authentic individuality and community. An attitude of reverence also stands as a prerequisite for a healthy attitude toward our natural environment. As Oppenheim describes the Roycean notion of reverence:

> A person who has what Royce calls "the true sense of life,"
> who reveres life and its relations, somehow senses within live
> relationships what the Psalmist felt--such a presence of the
> Author of Life that a reverend "fear of the Lord" stirs as the
> most appropriate response.[87]

While Oppenheim cites the Psalmist as a clear example of the reverence that marks the true sense of life, he does not limit this reverential sense to the biblical or any other religious tradition. The deeper sense of life can inspire reverence between spouses, lovers, friends and family members. Other awe-inspiring moments can be found:

> ...in authentic educational experiences, in deep interpersonal
> communications, in the genuine mutual trust of compacting
> business partners as together they face a risky future, in a
> scientific group's authentic search for further findings, and
> in an artist's creative in-touch-ness with his or her inmost
> genius.[88]

Oppenheim uses the qualifiers "authentic" and "genuine" to describe those experiences in which the deeper sense of life is present. Of course, the experiences described above in business, science, and even in families, often lack reverence.

Part of our modern problem in our relations with each other and with the natural environment shows up in the fact that the term "reverence" has lost much of its power. We hardly understand what it means to "revere" someone or something. To perceive reality as sacred means to experience life reverently; this means with a combination of fear and love. Rudolph Otto defines The Holy as *Mysterium tremendum et fascinosum.*[89] This is translated literally as the fearsome and fascinating mystery. The fear does not proceed from danger, but from a feeling of being overwhelmed. Love motivates us to approach the sacred with deep respect rather than to flee from it.

To approach the sacred means to seek a connection with Being and Goodness. The term "being" in the history of philosophy referred to a fundamental reality on which all experiences and thinking depends. In the traditional view, the truth of an idea consists of its correspondence with reality, that which *is*. The reality or being of an object might differ from its appearance. The question of what it means "to be" was considered the most important question in philosophy, and from the time of Aristotle the attempt to answer this question was called "metaphysics." Traditional metaphysics affirmed a unity connecting everything that exists. To the extent that something exists, it is good. *Evil consists of a lack of being that occurs when integrity is lost or missing.* For example, on the biological level, health means wholeness and sickness express the loss of wholeness and harmony. On the moral level, virtue is wholeness and vice is the failure to develop virtue.

Much of our modern philosophy has lost the very meaning of the words "being" and "good." In this modern view the verb "to be" has only the role of a copula, connecting a subject to predicate as in a proposition (S *is* P); the good is that which we subjectively perceive as pleasurable. The pizza is *good* means only that I like the pizza. This description, of course, does not include all of contemporary philosophy, but it sums up the metaphysical and ethical implications of philosophy of logical positivism[90] that dominated much of American academic philosophy in the middle of the twentieth century.[91] Logical positivism did not just "lose" the metaphysical meaning of being and good, but explicitly rejected it as obsolete. The positivist rejection of metaphysics still permeates much of academic thinking as well as popular culture.

We, in our Western technological society, have lost much of our capacity to appreciate the sacred and we need to take stock of what we have gained and also what we have lost. We cannot return to an earlier age any more than adolescents can recapture the "magic" of childhood. But we, as a society, can move ahead to a more mature relationship with reality.

The modern world-view was born in the Age of Reason and the Enlightenment, the seventeenth- and eighteenth-century movements in which scientific reasoning replaced religion and cultural tradition as the dominant force in human affairs. The description here does not take into account all thinkers of the 17th and 18th centuries, but describes the prevailing attitude, not only in academic philosophy, but in the worldview that shaped politics and economics. The modern age, inspired by the new attitude toward reason and the Enlightenment, generated science, technology, political democracy, and capitalism, and thereby provided us with an unprecedented personal liberty and a spectacular quantity and variety of goods.

But the modern worldview also caused a sense of emptiness that spawns many personal and political problems. Scientific technology has given us a degree of control over nature, along with the power and the arrogance to degrade our environment. The Enlightenment produced an ethics that is exclusively anthropocentric, meaning that we humans placed our selves at the center of the universe and valued everything else only in terms of how it helped or harmed us.

Some writers have traced disenchantment and the loss of the sacredness of nature back to the rise of Greek philosophy and Hebrew monotheism.[92] But certainly, the dissolution of enchantment accelerated in the seventeenth century with the loss of animism and sacramentality. Animism refers to the belief in a natural world that lives and teems with gods or spirits, and the sacramental view sees nature as a sign of God's presence and grace. Rene Descartes, almost universally cited as the father of modern philosophy, stands at least symbolically at the beginning of modernity, of the Enlightenment, and the end of the old order of holiness and enchantment.

Abandoning the traditional philosophy, Descartes proclaimed that he would replace the speculative ideas of scholasticism with a new philosophy that would make us the masters and possessors of nature:

> Instead of the speculative philosophy that is taught in the schools we can find a practical philosophy by means of which knowing the force and action of fire, water, air, the stars, the heavens, and all other bodies that environ us, as distinctly as we know the crafts of our artisans, we can in the same way employ them in all those uses to which they are adapted and thus render ourselves the masters and possessors of nature. [93]

Descartes, along with his contemporaries and successors who followed his mandate, provided us with an abundance of good things including science and technology without which we literally could not live. But there is a price to pay, and we are paying it. The price includes degradation of our natural environment and of our spirit.

The new philosophy fathered by Descartes changes the world from a living *Thou* to a dead *it*.[94] The modern world sees nature as an inanimate machine and the mechanistic view extends to our own body and to our social entities. The human mind becomes a detached observer and manipulator of the world. The disenchanted individual stands alone as an atomistic unit who interacts with other individuals through war, politics, or trade, depending on which method best secures his or her desires. We reduce everything in nature to quantifiable characteristics as befits a machine. We dismiss such subjective qualities as color, texture, and taste, as well as all feelings as secondary. Theologian Matthew Fox observes that in all of Descartes' writings about the natural world, the term "beauty" never comes up.[95]

The ethics of the Enlightenment focused only on human persons and human rights so that our duties were only to ourselves and other persons. As expressed by the most influential philosopher of the Enlightenment, Immanuel Kant, we are commanded by a categorical imperative to treat each person as an *end* also and not merely as a *means* to our ends. This solid but incomplete principle for dealing with persons leaves non-human nature in a devalued condition.

The disenchanted view pervades all aspects of life but especially the economy. Capitalism and her hostile younger sister, socialism, emerged as children of the Enlightenment. They hold in common the labor theory of value that John Locke articulated in the seventeenth century. Locke argued that things in nature belong to us all but have no value. We humans create value when we take things out of their natural state and mix them with our labor. The labor that goes into fashioning a product from nature makes that object valuable and it becomes "property" meaning one's own. We treat the whole non-human world from the minerals and fossil fuels under the ground to the highest of the non-human animals as if they have no value except as they can be used for human consumption or capital.

Socialism arose in response to the labor theory of value and the use of human labor as a commodity. Karl Marx expressed valuable insights, despite the mixed results of its application. Marx pointed out that private property has made us so stupid that we can think of something being ours only if we have it as an object to possess or consume or invest.[96] But Marx also accepted the labor theory of value and held that products have only the value that labor gives to them. Marx saw labor, and therefore ownership, as collective rather than private, but he did not go beyond the modern anthropocentric discounting of nature. Lenin's interpretation of Marx led to a devastating impact on the natural environment. The Soviet degradation of nature surpassed that of capitalism, which at least had some countervailing forces to check the power of industry.

It is not my intention to bash the Enlightenment and the technology of the modern era. We could not live without it, and I do not wish to bite the hand that feeds us. But perhaps we can look on it as we would an aging grandfather. We would not exist without him; we owe him gratitude, respect, and probably love. But we have to acknowledge that he can no longer sustain us or even himself. The Enlightenment and the science and technology that followed gave us a greatly improved material standard of living as well as enhanced individual rights, liberty, and opportunity. These are gains that most of us do not want to lose. The point of this brief summary of modern thought is not to advocate turning back to an idealized past. Rather, it suggests the need to move forward to a more comprehensive understanding that preserves and enhances our inter-human ethics, while surging ahead to a more integrative treatment of non-human nature. So, the point is to reflect on what our societal antecedents have done to nature and examine our present ethical requirements.

In the second half of the twentieth century, a developing environmental ethics served to awaken us to the intrinsic value of the non-human world, to the value of beauty, creation, and enchantment. In trying to reconstruct our ethical attitude, environmental ethics has given us a viewpoint from which we can begin to integrate nature into our ethical world. Of course, artists, poets, philosophers, and naturalists had found beauty and spiritual nourishment in nature for some time before the twentieth century, especially in the movement known as Romanticism, which began in the late eighteenth century as a reaction to rationalism of the Enlightenment described above.[97] Josiah Royce, living and writing before the emergence of environmental ethics, loved nature and hiked with his friend John Muir, one of the leading pioneers of American conservation.

In 1947, Aldo Leopold published *A Sand County Almanac,* in which he set out to develop a "land ethic." He argued that ethics develops over time and always involves the relations of individuals with each other and with their social organizations. The historical development of ethics entails the extension of areas of conduct governed by a sense of right and wrong. He shows examples of these extensions in the Mosaic Decalogue, the Golden Rule, and the emergence of political democracy.[98] The relation of human individuals to each other and to our organizations became more and more inclusive. But land is considered as mere property and not a part of life governed by ethical considerations. Leopold summed up the absence of a land ethic:

> No important change in ethics was ever accomplished without an internal change in our intellectual emphasis, loyalties, affections, and convictions. The proof that conservation has not yet touched these foundations of conduct lies in the fact that philosophy and religion have not yet heard of it. In our attempt to make conservation easy, we have made it trivial.[99]

Leopold believed that the next crucial stage in ethical development entails thinking of land, not as a commodity, but as a community deserving love and respect. He published these words in 1949, and since that time, many religious leaders, theologians, and philosophers have stepped up to teach the necessity of environmental care. Perhaps most notable is the 2015 Encyclical Letter of Pope Francis, *On Care for Our Common Home*. This work was welcomed by environmentalist regardless of their religious identification.

Leopold defined the guiding principle of a land ethic. "A thing is right when it tends to preserve the integrity, stability, and beauty of the biotic community. It is wrong when it tends otherwise." The emphasis on integrity, stability and beauty allows a land ethic to fit seamlessly with Royce's teleological harmony.

While the development of environmental ethics has prospered since 1947, there has been a strong backlash against it by those who limit ethical treatment to humans only. The inference drawn by the debunkers of environmental ethics goes: "If a creature cannot reason it has no duties; if it has no duties, it has no rights; if it has no rights, it has no value except as a means to the ends of humans." The goods of nature are reduced to a utilitarian value—-it can be good if and only if it is useful to us. A stark example of the disrespect for non-human nature that plagues much modern thinking shows up in an assessment by economist William Baxter. In determining whether any resources should be spent protecting the habitat of penguins, Baxter asserts, "Damage to penguins, or sugar pines or geological marvels is, without more, simply irrelevant...Penguins are important because people enjoy seeing them walk about rocks." [100] In this view, the non-human world has no meaning or value apart from its usefulness or pleasure for humans. So, if people find other entertainment more fun than watching penguins, the penguins are expendable.

Although Baxter exemplifies a logical extension of the notion that only humans have moral standing, his example may seem extreme, perhaps something that only an academic economist would say. The seeming strangeness of his position may be due to the fact that penguins resonate emotionally with many of us. We might not even know anyone who would willingly destroy the habitat of penguins simply because the economic value of their entertainment falls short of some other way to use their land. But in our real economy, we exhibit many practices that are morally equivalent to Baxter's values. One stark example can be found in extracting coal by mountain-top removal. This process involves blasting the mountain tops to rubble to expose the coal, while pushing the rocks layer by layer into the adjoining valleys, burying the streams and soil. This procedure is defended by politicians and news media in Appalachia on the grounds that it means cheaper electricity and preserves jobs in the mining industry. The eco-system itself as well as the once rich diversity of plants and animals count for nothing in the calculations of the decision makers.[101] The above description is not meant to deny the importance of energy and jobs. But the one-sided emphasis on monetary gain has made us as a culture blind to the well-being of the land and the people who live on it. Non-human living things fall outside of moral considerations all-together.

Another example of a cultural blindness to a land ethic can be found in the industrialization of agriculture. Just as coal-extraction practices make electricity cheaper, the practice of agribusiness makes food cheaper. As consumers, we seldom complain about low prices. But the real cost is hidden. As agrarian theologian Ellen Davis sums up the effect of our food production system:

> In this half century, (the system of petro-chemical based food production) has given North Americans probably the cheapest food in human history but at what cost? Changes in the composition of our top-soil (through heavy applications of chemicals); cultivation induced erosion, drastic narrowing of our seed base (through exclusive planting of a few hybrid strains); dangerous depletion of our water sources through over-pumping, as well as well as chemical poisoning caused by runoff.[102]

A Roycean approach would not deny or ignore the importance of the economic issues. Royce disdained "idealists" who refused to take the economic facts of life into account.[103] The quest for teleological harmony requires respect for all relations, economic as well as biological. Aldo Leopold's criteria of stability, integrity, and beauty can constitute a mid-twentieth century interpretation of Royce's notion of the good. Loyalty to loyalty requires that we integrate economic development with ecological conservation. The next section will deal with developing a more complete ethics.

Reverence for our Relations with Non-Human Nature

The consequence of the modern anthropocentric utilitarian view has been that we look at nature acquisitively and ask "What's in it for us?" instead of looking at it contemplatively and asking "What is it?" We might expect traditional religion to be a countervailing force against the lack of reverence for nature. Economist E. F Schumacher held that economics that acted as if the earth mattered would be a Buddhist economics in traditionally Buddhist countries such as Burma, but a Christian economics in Europe and the United States. But even Christian thought has to a large extent succumbed to the modern reduction of the non-human world in spite of the Gospel observation that the Creator cares about every sparrow. The exclusive anthropocentrism of the enlightenment contrasts sharply with an earlier natural law theory. St. Thomas Aquinas, for example, stated "God's goodness could not be adequately represented by one creature alone. God produced many and diverse creatures so that what was wanting to one in the manifestation of divine goodness might be supplied by another"[104] The neglect of the intrinsic goodness of the non-human world coincides with a shallow understanding of our own inner world. When the outer world is reduced to an object of quantitative calculation, the human is reduced to a calculator. As Schumacher observed, all traditional wisdom emphasizes self-knowledge as a condition for knowledge and the love of others:

> The Christian (and other) saints knew themselves so well that they could "see into" other beings. The idea that St Francis could communicate with animals, birds, and even flowers, must of course seem incredible to modern men who

have so neglected self-knowledge that they have difficulty communicating even with their wives. [105]

Farmer philosopher, Wendell Berry, in describing what he names "the sin of abstraction" argues that the Devil's work is found not in love of material things but in a love of quantification. A real lover of the material world would not sacrifice the natural environment by making profit maximization the only moral goal; the lover of quantification would.[106] Perhaps we can put a finer edge on Berry's point by saying that the sin is not quantification but reductionism that leaves out everything except quantification.

Berry, in developing a Christian approach to environmental care, cites the Buddhist notion of right livelihood and contends that Christianity has so far been inadequate in giving us a sense of right livelihood. One of the reasons, he argues, stems from the emphasis on other-worldliness. Christianity sees charity as a gift of God, but Berry points out that we need to learn how to put it into practice. Speaking from the view point of a farmer he asks; "How can you love your neighbor if you don't know how to build or mend a fence, how to keep your filth out of his water supply, and your poison out of his air?" He gives some suggestions of right livelihood.

> Real charity calls for the study of agriculture, soil husbandry, engineering, architecture, mining, manufacturing, transportation, the making of monuments and pictures, songs and stories. It calls not just for skill but for the study and criticism of skills, because in all of them a choice must be made: they can be used either charitably or uncharitably.[107]

It is clear that the charitable or desirable way to do each of these enhances the good of yourself, your neighbor, and the land on which all of us depend. To know exactly what the best way consists of requires careful study and criticism with an eye to the totality of our good and bad effects, and not just on the one narrow good of profit-making. We have a moral duty in the consumerist society to be not only ethical consumers but also ethical producers.

We find another sin of logical reduction that leads to moral wrongs in the all-or-nothing fallacy. Cartesian modernism has held that non-humans have no value in themselves because they are not rational beings with rights. On the opposite end of the spectrum, a form of environmentalism that mirrors modernism sees that non-human things have value and concludes they have rights in the literal sense in which humans have rights, and further, that all things with rights and values are equal. Dave Foreman, founder of *Earth First,* argues that the life of a human is not intrinsically more valuable than the life of a grizzly bear, and that apparent enemies like malaria are a valuable part of the biotic community. [108]

We can rant against this and make jokes about it, but our ethical thinking will advance beyond comical bickering only if we recognize that some things may have value, but other things have *more* value. As James Nash argued after rejecting the all-or-nothing approaches that holds that either animals have no value or that they have value equal to humans. "In contrast, a graded model claims that all creatures are entitled to 'moral consideration,' but not all have the same 'moral significance.'"[109] Nash attributes value to all forms of life but on an ascending value based on each organism's ability to experience and create value. If we can go beyond a humanistic hedonism, we can see that there is a value in all living things. According to environmental ethicist Holmes Rolston: "Something more than physical causes, even when less than sentience, is operating within every organism." [110] Bio-ethics must be based on a bio-logic. This means that we need to think from the premise that in every organism and in every bio-system there is an ontological reality with a definite order and program that demands respect. This does not mean that we owe them the same respect that we should show to humans or even to higher animals. We are not acting wantonly when we put our needs above the needs of other animals and plants as in eating food or combating disease. But we must recognize that living things have an intrinsic value that does not depend on whether they serve human wants and needs. We cannot live and "do no harm." But we can strive to minimize harm and to live with a sense of reverence and gratitude toward the living things that sustain us.

Ethics requires us as citizens to support public policy that protects and improves both the land and the people. Since technology moves constantly the best ideas as to how to do this will have changed from the time of this writing to the time that you are reading it. Therefore, it would not be appropriate to speculate on the exact way in which our use of energy ought to change. Currently it is not clear what will be the best way to power our production of electricity or our transportation, although it seems clear that we will want and need sources of power for both of these activities. We might cling to the current practice of burning massive amounts of fossil fuel including imported oil until the system breaks down completely. If the ethical analysis presented in this chapter is correct, then finding and implementing more environmentally friendly production and use of energy ought to be a priority of the government of the United States as well as that of all national governments. Since war contributes so much to pollution and destructive use of resources, along with the massive destruction of life and the unspeakable grief that it imposes on populations, avoiding and preventing war remains at the top of ethical imperatives. The technology for achieving a significant reduction of pollution as well as independence from foreign oil is available in concept. So far, we have not shown the political will to implement any solution.

One task of ethics is to remind us that our consuming as well as our producing material goods has effects beyond ourselves. We use our purchasing power ethically by being aware of our impact on ourselves, the producers, and the whole social and natural environment. In our work life we need to discover what the Buddhists call right livelihood. A desirable work life leads to greater integrity and integration. We have an unprecedented capacity for destruction but also an opportunity for building the human and biotic community. A major ethical mandate for us in the twenty-first century requires us to develop and live out a philosophical view that combines scientific and technological know-how with a reverence for our relationships with each other and with the natural world.

CHAPTER 7
Social and Economic Justice

Royce's ethical categories of autonomy, duty, and the good, as teleological harmony, can provide clarity and leadership in the area of social justice. But because the idea of social justice itself is so unclear and controversial, the bearing of Royce on this issue will be applied only after some preliminary work showing what is at stake in the discussion of social justice.

Definition of Social Justice and the Spectrum of Opinions

The mention of social and economic justice arouses controversy, not only in terms of what is right and wrong, but even in terms of what the concept means. Some even deny that the concept has any meaning. While the state of this subject requires some justification of the language used, we can begin with a working definition: "Economic justice is concerned with certain moral criteria for evaluating the distribution of economic goods in the material sense of wealth and income including the opportunities and social structure that undergird this distribution."[111] Economic justice can be taken as a sub-class of social justice, although by far the most important one. Social justice could also include non-material goods such as personal opportunities or access to political power, whether or not such opportunities and access have significant economic implications. General social justice and economic justice are so similar and woven into each other that whatever can be said of one can be said of the other in almost all instances. Some writers use the term "distributive justice" to indicate what others call economic justice. The following discussion will use "social justice" to include the definition of "economic justice" as defined above.

Another name for social justice, "distributive justice," evokes the question of how the material goods of the world should be distributed. The views on this issue vary from those who argue that the current situation is radically unfair, and that redistribution is a moral imperative to those who argue that the whole notion of economic justice is fraudulent and that no one has the right to distribute anything except his or her own property. A representative expression of the dismissal of economic justice by some conservatives is found in a column by retired economist Thomas Sowell: "What does 'economic justice' mean except that you want something that someone else produced, without having to produce anything yourself in return?"[112] The debate becomes unproductive when it settles into a dispute between the notion that economic justice means, on the one hand, re-distributing wealth to achieve equality, and on the other hand the complete rejection of economic justice. Most ethicists, as well as those who have responsibility for public policy, take a position somewhere between the two above extremes. The purpose of this first section consists of clarifying the meaning of social and economic justice and the reasoning that supports the various positions.

Is the present system just? When offered to a class of college students, or to a group of adults, my experience shows that this question can produce a lot of heat and unproductive opinions unless we can achieve some clarity on the meaning of justice. Some assume that justice means equality and point out that the current situation is patently unjust. Opponents of social justice agree that social justice means equality, and so they reject the notion of social justice as a theft against those who have earned wealth. Also, those who reject social justice often depict it as a disguise to increase the power of government.[113]

The whole notion of social justice requires clarification. Justice generally means the right distribution of benefits and burdens. Differences abound on the question of what constitutes "right distribution." As a step toward clarification, we can express the notion of justice as follows: "Every person should get what he or she deserves. No one in a society should be arbitrarily deprived of its benefits nor arbitrarily made to carry its burdens." The question remains as to what benefits and burdens, if any, belong to an individual simply by being a member of a society. Clearly, we do not all receive equal benefits or carry equal burdens. This fact of inequality does not necessarily constitute injustice, but it provides an opening into a better understanding. Taking factual inequality as a starting point, we ask whether any non-arbitrary reasons justify the unequal distribution of benefits and burdens. To refine the issue further we must ask: What differences among people are relevant to the question of distribution of goods? Are there relevant differences that account for the economic difference among people?

We see a spectrum of opinions between the libertarian view and the egalitarian view. Egalitarians favor a maximum of economic equality on the grounds that the concept of political equality, which has emerged and grown since the Enlightenment, ought to also pertain to the economic lives of people. Libertarians, drawing from another Enlightenment value, favor a maximum of freedom. Much of the ethical and political debate deals with how to balance these two goods, equality and liberty.

Extreme Views: Socialism and Libertarianism

Calling socialism an extreme view may sound like stacking the deck. But the reality of political discourse, at least in the United States in the late twentieth century and the early twenty-first century is that few politicians call themselves Socialists,[114] and opponents use the term "Socialist" only to smear an opponent. Nevertheless, by examining the meaning of socialism we can better understand the strengths and weaknesses of moderate views that approach or resemble socialism. There are several versions of socialism, but the one that had the most historical impact is that of Karl Marx, who called his political philosophy, "communism," although he did not intend the oppressive state-controlled society that emerged after the Russian revolution in 1917.[115]

Marx offered a Socialist ideal of justice—"From each according to his ability; to each according to his need." This statement can have many interpretations, but it helps to understand what Marx himself meant by it. Although he adamantly denied being Utopian, Marx described a communist society that bears no resemblance to the later realities of Stalinism and Maoism. In Marx's concept of a communist society, technology (he used the term "engines") would eliminate the mind-numbing and debasing jobs. Capitalist societies, he argued, drag their feet in development of technology because of the fear of unemployment and the ensuing social unrest. But in Marx's communist society everybody would have their needs met by the abundance produced by technology, and everybody would have a place in society.[116] The notion of everybody contributing to his or her ability rests on the notion that when people are not forced to perform "alienated labor" to feed themselves, they will naturally define and perform the work that suits their ability. A few examples will illustrate what I think Marx had in mind. Many people enjoy growing things, some like to build structures or furniture, others are attracted to mechanical and technological work. In this way society would get from each person according to his or her ability.

As far as needs, everybody obviously needs food, clothing, and shelter. Although we need medical care, the amount varies in everything from dental care to surgery. But in addition, there are specific needs. A carpenter, for instance, needs tools, a musician needs an instrument. So, Marx believed that in a communist society, everyone's needs would be met without depriving anyone else.

Like most thinkers who try to describe or prescribe the future, Marx got it wrong. A Marxian revolution never occurred in the developed capitalist countries, and the kind of communist society that Marx envisioned never arose anywhere. Further, capitalist countries enjoyed a spectacular success in the ability to produce economic goods. Marx's predictions of the future communist society still may have some value in an ethics book as models against which we can compare our actual and possible realities.

On the opposite end of the political spectrum stands the libertarian view of distributive justice. According to some libertarians, *the very concept of distributive justice is wrong* because it pre-supposes a distributor.[117] Personal moral responsibility consists only of refraining from fraud and violence, and the role of government should be limited to protecting citizens from fraud and violence. People have negative rights, e.g., the right not to be killed or robbed; they do not have the right to be fed or given anything. According to this view, taxing one person to provide for another is theft, and makes the tax-payer a slave for a portion of his or her working year.

Given the libertarian argument against social justice, and the emotional appeal that it has on all of us who like to think of ourselves as independent, social justice stands in need of defense. Some libertarians and conservatives refuse to even hear arguments for social justice because they assume that if there were such a thing, it would mean taking money from those who earned it and distributing it equally to all including those who earned nothing.

Those who argue against the concept of "distribution" base their argument, nevertheless, on a concept of distribution. Arguing for the status quo is an argument for a particular distribution, namely, the way things are, and will be if left to "market forces." Libertarians usually argue that taxes are too high and social programs should be pared back, or better yet, eliminated. This paring back of social safety nets would constitute "redistribution" as more of the wealth would move from the bottom of the economic ladder toward the top. Those who promote such redistribution should show why their proposals can be considered more just than those of their opponents, rather than denying that their ideas constitute a redistribution.

Friedrich Hayek, in his 1944 classic, *The Road to Serfdom* presented an influential argument against social justice, which he called distributive justice. His assumptions are that distributive justice aims at economic equality, and that it violates the "Rule of Law." He argues that The Rule of Law treats everybody equally, gives no person or group special privileges, and protects individual from interference by arbitrary government. He states:

> A necessary and only apparently paradoxical, result of this is that formal equality before the law is in conflict, and in fact incompatible, with any activity of the government deliberately aiming at material or substantive equality of different people, and that any policy aiming directly at a substantive ideal of distributive justice must lead to the destruction of the Rule of Law.[118]

Since individuals are different in such things as ability, willingness to work, willingness to take risks, and luck, equality before the law will inevitably lead to inequality of economic status. Hayek argues that material equality can be achieved only by treating people unequally by government intervention. Hayek's argument rests on the assumption that social justice must mean equality and that any difference of treatment among individuals is arbitrary and so violates the Rule of Law. In the following I will make the argument for a concept of social justice that rejects both of these assumptions. But first some more moderate views of social justice can help clarify the issue.

Moderate Views: Liberal and Conservative

Unlike Marx, who thought in terms of a revolution that would end the "bourgeois" values of the Enlightenment, John Rawls developed an egalitarian theory that is in the tradition of liberal democracy. He believes that we can discern a just social order by a thought experiment in which we construct a "veil of ignorance." Behind the imaginary veil of ignorance, none of us knows where we stand on the social and economic ladder and which policies would benefit us most. In such a case, we each, in our own rational self-interest, would favor the distribution that would be the most acceptable, regardless of what our position turned out to be. This does not necessarily mean that we would favor a pure equality, but that we would oppose any *arbitrary inequality*. Inequalities are justified if they provide for the benefit of all.[119] An acceptable inequality would be one that stood in the best interest of everyone, especially those on the lowest rung. An example of such inequality would be an entrepreneur whose accumulated capital provides jobs and incomes to others.

Some defenders of capitalism argue that the inequalities brought about by a free market, are justified by the fact that those who receive more are precisely those who contribute more as judged by the market. A capitalist view of justice, playing on the Marxian principle of "From each according to his ability..." states, "From each according to his willingness to participate in the system; to each according to his success in participating." [120] In capitalism, the principle is not simply from each according to his or her ability, but from each according to his or her ability *and* willingness to contribute. The willingness consists not only of a general willingness to work, but to do a particular kind of work, or develop a particular kind of skill, or a particular entrepreneurial idea. For example, one person might learn a construction trade such as brick-laying or carpentry and wish to work in construction; another may want to start a small business such as a restaurant; a third might want to work in management for a corporation. If each of them achieves what they set out to do, they will receive a wage, profit, or salary, and the economy will benefit from their particular skill and work. Anyone may fail because of lack of ability or because their skills are not needed at a given time. In the example above, a business recession may lead to a loss of livelihood for the construction worker, the restaurant owner, and the corporate manager. According to the capitalist or free-market theorist, such a loss is a misfortune but not an injustice.

The terms "capitalist" and "libertarian" often overlap and sometimes are used interchangeably. For example, Ayn Rand and her followers identify their economic philosophy as "capitalism," but it coincides with what is generally called libertarianism. Of course, not all capitalists are libertarians, nor do they necessarily reject the notion of using public funds to help people in need. While the libertarians reject the notion of social justice, a capitalist may defend the value of social justice but affirm that the free market is the most just distributor of wealth. Such capitalists base their arguments on the fact that a person's ability and willingness to work create wealth not only for that person, but for the whole society. The successful capitalists, while becoming rich, also provide jobs, products, and tax revenue. Without the activity of the capitalist, everyone would be less well-off including those who are relatively poor.

A Reasonable Approach to Economic Justice

Given the libertarian argument that no one has the right to distribute any property other than his or her own, and given the capitalist argument that the market can distribute goods more justly than any other human mechanism, is there a need for a separate category of economic justice? In fact, there are two moral principles that create a mandate for clear thinking on economic justice. These principles are the notion that *the goods of the earth belong to all*, and the notion *of moral equality,* meaning that every human being has the right to be treated with respect. Merely stating these principles does not necessarily disprove the argument that a free market provides the best distribution, nor does it prove that any existing inequalities are unjust. But the principles do require us to examine what constitutes economic justice and to work toward its implementation.

One of the strongest arguments for economic justice, if not for economic equality, stems from the notion that the goods of the earth belong to all. This argument did not arise in pre-modern times when the land was thought to belong to the king, or to a feudal strongman who was literally a land lord. This notion changed drastically with the Enlightenment when thinkers such as Thomas Hobbes, argued that the natural law directed each person to do whatever would ensure his own survival and this might mean controlling as much of the land as possible.[121] John Locke later argued explicitly that things in their natural state belonged to all. But he laid down the basis for private property by arguing that things have value only when mixed with human labor. Since the work of our hands is ours individually, the product of that work is also ours as private property. This principle established both the basis for justice and the approval of inequality. Inequalities result from some persons working more effectively than others thus creating more value. But the inequalities have to be justified since the goods begin by belonging equally to all.

A second Enlightenment idea that leads to a notion of economic justice is the moral equality of all human beings. In the seventeenth and eighteenth centuries, the notion of equality referred to moral, political, and legal equality, but not to economic equality. But if we are by nature equal as human beings, some justification must be given if economic inequality is to be morally acceptable and not merely a result of the more powerful grabbing more than they deserve. While few people today argue for a simple equality, we differ widely among ourselves as to how much inequality can be tolerated, and on what grounds. The libertarians argue that any inequality is justified as long as there is no force or fraud involved.

Some conservative writers argue that since justice is a virtue, and virtues are habits that reside only in individuals, the notion of any kind of social justice is meaningless. F. A. Hayek makes this argument. Michael Novak, agreeing in principle with Hayek, suggests a way to keep social justice as a meaningful concept. Novak agrees that justice is a virtue that must be attributed to individuals, but contends that if several individuals work together to improve the common good of their community, such cooperation can be called social justice.[122] Novak's view, like Hayek, rejects the notion of social justice as part of public policy.

I contend, to the contrary, that although individual and cooperative habits are essential parts of justice, and that problems that can be solved by individuals and communities should not be taken over by government, nevertheless, there is a place for public policy that can rightly be called social justice. We can discern *injustice* in the structures and laws of society, and therefore we can define what, in the public sphere, constitutes *social justice*. Some more obvious historical examples of social injustice include slavery and discrimination. But others examples include omissions, such as the failure on the part of the public sector to protect individuals from the results of environmental destruction, dangerous or exploitative working conditions, and inferior educational opportunities.

Any person's concept of justice is based on his or her concept of *what a human being is* and why we should be concerned with treating each person justly. A Roycean view of the human individual affirms each person's absolute worth as a potential member of the universal community. Our capacity for membership in any genuine community rests on the fact that we are rational, free, capable and in need of meaningful work, communal, and needing the opportunity to realize our full physical, intellectual, emotional, and spiritual capacity. Therefore, any structure or practice that inhibits a person from realizing his or her human nature is unjust, and that which promotes it is just. Equality as a moral task can mean doing whatever we can to assure that each person has an opportunity to realize his or her human potential. This entails much more than removal of obstacles such as discrimination. Real equality of opportunity must include providing the conditions that make realization possible. If a person has the ability and desire to develop productive skills, but lacks the opportunity, does this constitute an injustice? The role of justice lies in determining what each person has the right to and who has the obligation to provide it.

Integrity and Integration in the Economy

The key to understanding social justice consists in recognizing that we are mutually interdependent. Each of our lives has an impact on countless people of whom we are not aware, and the activities of other people impact each of us. No one in isolation and relying on only his or her own native ability can become an engineer, an accountant, a steamfitter, a golfer, or a musician. All of these things require physical and social structures and involve imitation and intense education, both formal and informal. While those who deny social justice may agree that we have an obligation as individuals to people whom we immediately affect, our universal mutual interdependence requires us to also pay attention to how we collectively impact other people through our political, economic, educational, and civil institutions.

The attempt to articulate a well-integrated approach to social justice can benefit from a study of classical American philosophers. In their book, *Rethinking Business Ethics: A Pragmatic Approach*, Sandra Rosenthal and Rogene Buchholz draw not from Royce, but from other classical pragmatists such as John Dewey, G. H. Mead, Charles Sanders Peirce, and William James. Rosenthal and Buchholz argue that nearly all modern and contemporary ethical theories begin with a questionable premise that impedes our understanding of justice, especially social justice.[123] These authors contend that, "Once the individual is taken as an isolatable unit, then the individual and the community become pitted against each other in an ultimately irreconcilable tension." [124] Ethics requires as a starting point, a view of *individuals as essentially social as well as autonomous.* The premise that they reject holds that atomistic individuals live and work prior to their affiliation with other atomistic individuals. Morality, in this view, consists in finding the right way to live with other individuals and collective groups that we call society.

The libertarian view, which agrees with Ayn Rand that selfishness is a virtue, and sees the individual as radically autonomous and morally constrained by nothing except the equal rights of other atomistic individuals exemplifies the modern view most starkly. But even the Kantian duty ethics, which requires that we respect all rational beings as "ends in themselves" and that we follow rules that we can affirm as universally binding, presents ethics as following the correct rules for individuals in dealing with other individuals. Utilitarianism holds that the greatest good consists of happiness, and requires that we extend the promotion of happiness to all feeling beings, and affirms that selfishness constitutes one of the greatest sources of unhappiness. But the pursuit of happiness resides in each individual.

Any society that excludes some part of the population either by design or by neglect, to that extent, suffers a deficiency of justice. Although giving a person a handout, by the state or by private charity, beats letting the person starve or freeze, such largess falls short of justice. The goal of achieving a just society requires that we, individually and collectively, do what we can to assure that each person can take a productive social and economic role. To achieve this level of inclusiveness would be very difficult, if not practically impossible. Nevertheless, it is a standard against which we can measure our level of success and failure at building a just society.

The theme of this book is purposive integration or "teleological harmony." We can rate our society as a just society to the extent that each and every individual has a place in the society that enables them to develop their full human potential. There will probably always be misfits, sociopaths, and criminals. The question of social justice requires that we ask whether we are giving each person sufficient opportunity to be productive and prosperous, and how we treat those who reject or neglect the opportunities that are provided. Whether their problem is physical, psychological or moral, they still belong to the human community. We can move to seek ways to incorporate them, although there is no guarantee of success. Or we can reject or neglect them with the self-assurance that their problem is their fault, not ours. As in every aspect of ethics, we can integrate or disintegrate.

CHAPTER 8
Ethical Issues Involving the Beginning of Life

The experience of an unwanted pregnancy is an actual reality for many couples and a potential reality for many more. Sometimes, tragically and unfairly, the woman stands alone to face this issue. There are wide-ranging moral beliefs on this issue. Some believe that the unborn is a part of the woman's body, and the decision to keep it or not depends only on her wishes. Others maintain that the unborn is a human whose life should be protected with the same laws that protect you and me from murder. In this chapter, I hope to examine the assumptions behind each of these positions, to understand why people in the same society can be so far apart, and to see if there is any chance of finding common ground where all sides can work together.

What moral principles would guide you in determining how to respond to an unwanted pregnancy for yourself or someone who confided in you? Are there circumstances that would change the appropriateness of your decision? Do you believe that the decision to keep or to abort the embryo or fetus should be governed by law? Should it be the private decision of the pregnant woman?

The Divisiveness of the Abortion Issue

Few moral issues divide the American people as much as the issue of abortion. Proponents on each side, usually referring to themselves as "pro-life" or "pro-choice," passionately affirm that they stand for the morally right cause. The discussion in ethics courses and books generally comes down to trying to analyze the arguments of each side to determine which is right and which is wrong. Here, too, we will examine some of the key arguments of each side. But the theme of this book emphasizes that ethical thinking must go beyond choosing sides and must try to nourish the good while respecting all parties involved in the debate. Achieving the good as teleological harmony presents a task much more difficult than choosing sides, and may bring the wrath of both sides down on our heads.

The story of a young woman in the 1980s clearly illustrates the problem. She became pregnant as a teenager and, since she held "pro-choice" views, she considered an abortion. However, after serious thought, she decided to have the baby. After the birth of her daughter, whom she dearly loves, she took a firm "pro-life" position. Because she understood both sides, and because she had considerable organizational skills, she thought she could play a key role in creating "common ground." Since both sides profess to care deeply about the well-being of young women, could they not work together to provide education to prevent unwanted pregnancies in the first place? Further, when girls become pregnant, they need medical, financial and emotional support regardless of what decision they make. So, the young lady approached each side to bring them together in a common cause.

Her position seemed reasonable, perhaps too reasonable for the climate in which she tried to realize her plan. When she approached a "pro-life" organization, she was told that although they admired her effort, the pro-life advocates simply could not cooperate in any way with people who advocated killing the unborn. The "pro-choice" leaders whom she approached expressed anger at her for supporting people who wanted to deprive women of the right to control their own reproduction. Neither side was willing to search for a common ground. The young lady was not trying to do the impossible; she just came on the scene too early to be successful.[125] In the following, we will look at the issue of abortion by taking an honest look at the arguments for both positions with the immediate goal of understanding. Next, we will look deeper to see if any reconciliation is possible without a betrayal of principle.

The Status of the Unborn

To understand another person's attitude toward abortion, or even to understand our own attitude, we have to know what he or she thinks about the status of an unborn human embryo and fetus. Is an unborn human a person who has the same right to life as you and I, or is it something else? This question marks one of the parting-of-ways in which each side not only believes in the correctness of its position but also believes that any honest person would acknowledge their correctness as obvious. Some pro-life advocates think that everyone knows that killing the unborn is wrong, but do it anyway out of convenience. Pro-choice advocates, in turn, charge that the pro-life movement is simply a way to enforce a conservative sexual morality. There may be some individuals on each side for whom these charges are true, but we will not make any moral progress as a society until all parties learn to understand the legitimate claims of the other.

We can begin to make headway by asking, what is an unborn human? Does it have the right to life? Why do you and I have the right to life, and when did we acquire this right? Did we acquire the right at conception, birth, or some other time? The disagreement on abortion stems from the disagreement on these questions.

Two distinct questions regarding abortion require clarification, questions that both sides often confuse. The first and most basic question, stated as a moral question, asks if abortion is right or wrong. Or more precisely, whether it can be right in some situations and wrong in others, and what would make it right or wrong? The second, the legal and political question, derives from the first. Should abortion be outlawed? Outlawing abortion would require a constitutional amendment or a seismic shift in the opinion of the Supreme Court.

This issue has played a prominent role in politics, including presidential politics since the 1980s. [126]

The moral question asks how a person ought to deal with an unwanted pregnancy. This question may impose itself not only on a woman who becomes pregnant and her partner, but also on any of us in terms of friends, relatives, or persons who seek our counsel. The legal and political question asks what kind of public policy we ought to work for regarding the legality of abortion. The following paragraphs will present strong arguments for and against abortion followed by a summary of the majority opinion in Roe v. Wade, which made abortion legal in all fifty states. This section will conclude with an ethical assessment of the present legal and political issues regarding abortion.[127]

Basing the Right to Life on Biological Humanness

A very strong traditional argument defending the right to life of the unborn comes from John T. Noonan, a highly respected California judge and legal scholar.[128] Noonan argues that

to protect the rights of all people from arbitrary definitions, there must be a non-arbitrary definition of human life. In the past, even the very recent past, people were excluded from the full protection of law because of arbitrary considerations such as race, ethnicity, gender, and physical and mental deficiencies. An arbitrary definition depends on the opinion of the definer. A non-arbitrary definition stems from the very nature of the thing being defined, in this case a human being.

Noonan asserts that *any being conceived by human parents is human.* This definition has momentous impact on the issue of abortion since it implies that human rights begin at conception. Noonan sets out to show that any other definition is arbitrary. Those who approve abortion contend that the right to life begins at birth. This position coincides with the legal standing of the born and unborn in the United

States at present. The law considers killing a baby the day it is born as homicide; killing it in the womb is not legally homicide. But Noonan argues that a baby is essentially the same on the day before it is born as it is immediately after it is born. The differences are place, being outside the womb instead of inside, and breathing with its own lungs instead of receiving oxygen through the umbilical cord. If it is wrong to kill a newborn baby, as nearly everyone agrees, then no rational argument can be made for killing it the day before it is born.

There is no non-arbitrary point between conception and birth that would serve to distinguish a human individual from what is not a human individual. The only valid candidate for the beginning of human life is conception. Although each ovum and sperm are alive, the ovum has a relatively small chance of being fertilized, and each sperm has an infinitesimally small chance of fertilizing an ovum. At conception, the odds of survival for this sperm and this ovum, as a new being, increase astronomically. Moreover, the genetic code is set for the growth and development of a new person. No other event in life comes close to this in biological significance. Therefore, human life ought to be defined and protected from the time of conception.

A possible response to Noonan would point out that although there is no single moment during gestation that would constitute a discernible difference between a person and a non-person, from one day to another, there is a great difference between a newly conceived embryo and a developed fetus. Such an argument can be construed to justify an early term abortion but not a late-term abortion.

Basing the Right to Life on Personhood

If a pro-abortion argument does not wish to leave the right to life open to arbitrary definitions, it must face Noonan's logic and show why it is wrong to kill you or me, but not wrong to kill an embryo or fetus. An argument to justify abortion would have to show that our right to life is based on something other than our genetic humanness. One such argument comes from philosopher Mary Ann Warren.[129]

There can be no question that the unborn, from the moment of conception is alive and genetically human. So, the issue does not consist of biological disagreements; both sides are looking at the same embryological information. The real question, which is a moral question, cannot be settled by bringing in more biological data. The moral question asks whether we have the right to life because of our human conception, as Noonan argued, or because of our "personhood."

The distinction between "human" and "person" may sound absurd to some, because all of the persons whom we know are humans and all of the humans whom we know are persons. In our life experience they appear inseparable. Warren, however, argues that the term "human" has two closely related but distinct meanings. In a biological sense we are human, as Noonan argued, if we are conceived of human parents. Warren argues that our right to life is based on being human in the moral sense, i.e., on being a person, rather than just in the biological sense. Anyone who wants to understand the position of those who permit abortion, whether they agree with it or not, must understand the distinction that some such as Warren makes between a biological human and a human person.

If a distinction opens up between a biological human and a person, the key question asks what constitutes a person. We who take part in this discussion have certain qualities that serve as the basis for respecting us as persons. These qualities include consciousness, self-consciousness, reasoning, language, and self-motivated activity. Although not all of these characteristics are required to be a person, a being who had all of them would clearly be a person; a being who had none of them would not be a person.

Our law and common morality does not consider non-human animals as persons although they clearly possess consciousness and some ability to communicate. Warren argues that if we found non-human animals that had all of the qualities that constitute personhood, we would be obligated to treat them as persons. Since the beginning of philosophical thinking, traditional thinkers defined humans as rational animals. It is rationality that sets us apart from other animals and confers a legal right to life that we deny to the rest of the animal kingdom. So, if an animal of a different biological species shows that it can reason, we are compelled to treat it as a "rational animal" with all of the rights and privileges that we attribute to our fellow humans. I, for one, can find no fault with this argument. On the other hand, a human who has suffered brain death and whose body is kept alive for organ transplants is biologically alive and human, but not considered a person. Surgeons may remove vital organs because the "person" is already considered dead.

These examples show that biological humanness constitutes neither a necessary nor sufficient condition for personhood. We can at least imagine a person who is not human and a human who is no longer a person. Thus, Warren concludes that the fetus, while biologically human, is not a person. If her argument stands, then abortion does not morally constitute homicide. Warren grants that the unborn has the potential for personhood. But she concludes further that the desire of the mother, an actual person, to end her pregnancy, overrides any right that may be attributed to the potential person.

When Warren published her article, she was confronted with the issue of infanticide. Critics pointed out that by her reasoning, an infant would not rank as a person because it has no more characteristics of a person than does a fetus. The logic of her argument seems to condone infanticide. Warren apparently found the implications of her theory to be troubling. She did not wish to make an argument for infanticide, but her own logic led to that conclusion. She faced a dilemma. If her logic is right, then so is infanticide. But if infanticide is wrong, then there is a fatal flaw in her logic. She escaped the dilemma by holding fast to her position on abortion while providing a different argument against infanticide.

She answered that it is wrong to kill an infant because there are people, especially adoptive parents, who want the infant and would be distressed by its destruction. Even people who are not looking to adopt a child would be horrified at the prospect of killing unwanted children. The desire of those who want to protect the infant overrides the wish of anyone who wants its destruction including the mother. While Warren argues that a woman's right to her own body overrides the right of the potential person as well as the right of others who wish to protect the fetus, she concedes that once the baby is born, the mother has no compelling interest that would justify killing the baby.

The contrast between Noonan and Warren exemplifies the division on the issue. The question is whether we have the right to life because of our biological humanity or because of our personhood which includes self-consciousness and rationality. Critics of Warren often employ the "slippery slope" argument. One example showed up in the question of infanticide. If it is all right to kill a fetus, why not condone killing unwanted babies? Further, what can prevent killing children and adults who are deficient in rationality and ability to communicate? Advocates of abortion do not condone such killing of born humans, but the critics argue that by permitting abortion, we cross a line by allowing for an arbitrary definition of a human person.

A second criticism against Warren's position charges that even if we grant that an unborn is not a person in the full moral and legal sense, it is certainly a potential person. Warren agrees that it is a potential person but contends that the rights of an actual person, the mother, override the rights of this potential person. Her argument stands if she is talking about the life of an actual person and the life of a potential person. But does it follow that the convenience of the mother overrides the life of the unborn?

Basing the Right to Life on Having a Future[130]

While the Noonan-Warren difference exemplifies the main issue of the debate, Don Marquis developed an argument against abortion that has the interest of both sides. Marquis bases the case against abortion on the fact that the fetus has a future. We will examine this argument by first clarifying his premises. A basic moral axiom affirms that it is wrong to kill *us*. We must ask why it is wrong. If unborn humans are in the same category as we are with respect to the value of their lives, then it is also wrong to kill the unborn. The issue consists of the question, what makes it wrong to kill us?

Several answers could be given such as that killing a person causes sorrow to the friends and family of the victim. This is not a sufficient reason to explain the universal ban on murder because we consider it wrong to kill even a person whom nobody likes. Some might argue that it is wrong because it is illegal. But few would be willing to allow legislators to determine who does and does not have the right to life. Of course, most pro-life advocates affirm, with Noonan, that it is wrong to kill us because we are human. But Warren and most advocates of the permissibility of abortion do not concede that genetic humanness is sufficient to support the right to life.

Marquis offers an alternative reason why it is wrong to kill us. Our right to life, he argues, rests on the fact that we have a future. We value our future more than anything, and so the greatest loss that anyone can suffer is the loss of his or her future. "The loss of one's life deprives one of all the experiences, activities, projects, and enjoyments that would otherwise have constituted one's future."[131] Therefore killing someone is wrong because killing a person inflicts one of the greatest possible losses on the victim. Killing a person takes away not only the future that the person values now but also the future that he or she will come to value. Non-human animals live in the present, and animal rights advocates argue that it is wrong to deprive them of their present enjoyment. Without passing judgement of the animal-rights argument, killing animals is different from killing humans because animals do not have a consciousness that extends beyond the present. They may be alive for years to come, but they do not have plans, projects and hoped for experiences and projections that constitute having a future. Even if we protect the lives of animals, they will not have a future; they will have a prolonged and hopefully enjoyable present.

The fact that our future constitutes our greatest treasure can be seen in the attitude that we have toward our own death and that of other people. We know that those who face a premature death because of cancer or AIDS consider the imminence of their death to be an extreme misfortune. Their distress comes from knowing that their future will be cut short. When a person dies prematurely, the grief that we feel stems from the loss of experiences and achievements that had constituted that person's future. So much potential is unactualized. With people close to us, the grief is compounded by the impoverishment of our own future that we would have shared with them.

Since the unborn human has a future, we inflict great harm if we destroy its future.

Abortion is therefore wrong for the same reason that killing us is wrong. The opponents of Marquis may argue that a human does not have a future until that point in early childhood when he or she knows that there is a future — "When my birthday comes..." "When I get big..." The question is whether a being can have a future before it knows it has a future. Marquis argues that it does, because biologically it is on track to becoming a human person with a future. Our own future contains not only the things that we currently hope for, but those things of which we are currently unaware but which will become hoped for experiences and achievements. So, the future and the knowledge of the future await the unborn, and to deprive them of that future is a serious moral wrong.

Roe v. Wade, January 22, 1973

The legal status of abortion in the United States was defined on January 22, 1973, by the U. S. Supreme Court in the case known as Roe v. Wade.[132] A woman who was denied an abortion under Texas Law allowed a group of "pro-choice" attorneys to use her case under the fictitious name of Jane Roe.[133] Wade was the attorney for Dallas County.

In January 1973 the United States Supreme Court declared the Texas statute unconstitutional, hence all similar state laws were nullified, and abortion, which was already legal in some states, became legal in all fifty states. The majority opinion was written by Justice Harry Blackmun. In summary, the majority opinion states the following. At one time abortion was illegal in all states, but was not defined as homicide. State laws forbidding abortion were based on three reasons:

1. To protect morality by not allowing people to have sex without consequences.

2. To protect women from a dangerous procedure.

3. To protect the unborn.

By 1973 there was no longer much support for the first reason. Regarding the second reason, abortion had become much safer and would be safer yet if it were legal. The third reason is the contentious one.

The key legal question asks, "When does life begin?" In posing this question, Blackmun was referring to a legal definition of human life. Of course, the unborn is alive and human in a biological sense. But Blackmun argued that there is no consensus in this country on when a human being acquires the right to life. Of the three main religious groups, the Catholic Church and some others hold that the right to life begins at conception; those who practice the Jewish faith, for the most part, believe that it begins with birth; Protestantism covers a wide spectrum of views. Of course, many Americans subscribe to other religions or to no religion.

Blackmun defines the legal issue as a conflict between the interest of the state and the rights of individuals. The conflict at hand is the "right to privacy" versus the state's interest in protecting pre-natal life. Blackmun argues that although the state's interest in protecting unborn life is legitimate, it does not over-ride a fundamental individual right such as privacy. But the right to privacy, while fundamental, is not absolute. If the state has a compelling interest, it may over-ride a fundamental right.

At the time of conception, the state's interest is legitimate, but not compelling. After the first trimester, the state may claim a compelling interest in regulating abortion to assure its medical safety. The legitimate interest in pre-natal life increases as the fetus's potential to be born increases. At some point the state's legitimate interest becomes "compelling." Blackmun defined this point as the point of viability, when the fetus could live outside the womb. He noted that according to medical opinion, the fetus achieves viability between 24 and 28 weeks. At this stage, the state may regulate and even prohibit abortions.

Roe v. Wade has been challenged several times, but as of 2022, it is still the current ruling of the United States Supreme Court, which is the final arbiter on the interpretation of the Constitution. Those who wish to make abortion illegal have two avenues open. First, they could hope for the appointment of justices to the Supreme Court who would reverse Roe v. Wade after more than forty-five years. Due to recent appointments, it has become increasingly likely that state-wide bans on abortion will be permitted once again. Or second, they could attempt to amend the Constitution so that killing the unborn is explicitly prohibited.

Searching for Common Ground

The abortion issue cannot be resolved by debate. Arguments on the abortion issue as well as most other ethical issues are designed to support a position rather than to arrive at a logical conclusion. The pro-life argument begins with the premise that the unborn, from conception, is a human being with the right to life. Deliberately killing an innocent human being is always wrong and should be prohibited by law, just as killing a born human is prohibited. But those who advocate the permissibility of abortion deny the major premise that the unborn is a person with the right to life. As stated above, they do not deny that the unborn is biologically alive and human, but contend that it is only a potential person. The argument is usually mired in an all-or-nothing dichotomy. Either the unborn is as much a person as you or I, and so abortion should be considered as murder, or it is only part of the mother and has only the value that she gives to it.

The two sides appear to be irreconcilable, so that one side is right, the other wrong. Advocates of each side may take comfort in knowing that they have chosen the right and each side can be fiercely loyalty to its own cause, and seek the complete defeat of its opponent. A Roycean ethic seeks reconciliation and loyalty to loyalty. The difficulty for either side to interpret the issue in a way that allows it to see some good in its opponent's cause makes the project seem impossible, even in theory. Belief in the sanctity of human life from the beginning of pregnancy, and belief in the inviolability of a woman to determine her own reproductive destiny, seem to be contradictory non-negotiable stands. This is the way the issue presents itself, especially in the political arena.

Much of our thinking about the unborn reflects the thinness of modern thought that also shows up in the environmental issue. We have not shaken off the Enlightenment notion that the world is divided between rational human minds and inert matter. The language of rights, "right to life" or "right to choose," eclipses the more subtle language of duty and reverence for all of the relations of life. The divisive debate blinds us from appreciating the reality of the growth from embryo to person. But a full reverential appreciation must also realize the life of the potential mother, not just her biological life, but her full human historical life. Over many years of teaching ethics, I observed that young women, even those who are pro-life, see an appalling disconnect between the political move to make abortion illegal and the plight of a pregnant woman.

To contend that a woman should have a legal choice and that, with few exceptions, having a baby is the right moral choice recognizes the deepest moral ideals of each side. Some advocates of one or the other position may consider this as a contradiction. But it does not constitute a contradiction to say that a woman should have a choice, but to affirm that life is the right choice. Sustaining such a position is much more difficult than taking sides in the all-or-nothing debate.

In fairness to the reader, I will conclude this chapter with my own position on the moral and political reflection on this difficult issue without claiming to have any privileged insight. The unborn has an inherent value and should be protected by education, awareness of the greatness of life, a sense of community and solidarity with poor single pregnant women. This message is not heard in the present political climate. Before Roe v. Wade, abortion was already legal in some states. If the Supreme Court permits states to prohibit abortion, it might be prohibited in some states, but not all. There would almost certainly be an underground abortion business. The abortionists would not necessarily be sinister characters "in dark alleys with coat hangers." More likely, they would be trained professionals who believe in the right to abortion. Practitioners would become heroes and, if arrested, martyrs in the eyes of people who favor abortion. Abortion would be portrayed by many as a noble cause, and there would be no way to ever teach the sanctity of the unborn human life. The chance would be lost forever to form a common ground to foster the good of all pregnant women and unborn humans.

If the pro-life advocates let go of the political issue of trying to make abortion illegal, the pro-abortion side would lose its issue. They could no longer rally behind "the right to choose" and everyone would have to ask what makes a good choice given the reality of unborn human life. The pro-life/pro-choice dichotomy can be overcome. Activists on both sides can agree on the goal of averting unwanted pregnancies. In the case of a pregnancy, there would still be disagreement as to whether having a baby is the only good choice or merely the better choice. But all can agree on the need to protect the health of the mother, and if she is having the baby, to protect it from conception to birth and through childhood. Especially in cases of underage single women, both sides can agree that adoption may be a viable choice. Loyalty to life itself and reverence to the relations of life can take us a long way from the current divisive standoff.

CHAPTER 9
Ethical Issues Involving the End of Life

Defining the Ethical Issues of Caring for the Dying

Loyalty and reverence for the relations of life almost always prompt us to foster life, to act in ways that promote living, thriving, and flourishing. But mortality looms as one of our defining characteristics. How do we deal with our own impending death and the deaths of those whom we love, revere, and share loyalties? The most obvious and general answer is that we treat them lovingly, reverently, and loyally. But what about death itself? Do we resist it to the last breath, accept it, or even promote it? These questions evoke another important and controversial issue in our society, the question of euthanasia.

In planning for our own death and in dealing with the death of those whom we love, we can look to the first of the four ethical questions, which have been a major theme of this book. *What is desirable as opposed to merely desired?* We may *desire* to cling to a loved person even if it means prolonging her suffering and death. Is this a loving act? Or we may *desire* that the dying process may be shortened so that we can get on with our own life. Such a desire sounds calloused, yet many of us might succumb to it in times of fatigue and stressful care-giving. While it might be true that nothing fully prepares us for a death, we can mitigate the difficulty by thinking clearly before death confronts us. "What is the most desirable way to handle our own death and that of those who we love?" These considerations evoke another important and controversial issue in our society, the question of euthanasia.

The term "euthanasia," derived from the Greek word for "good death," refers to killing a person for that person's benefit. In almost every case in which anyone argues for its permissibility, the benefit to the person means sparing him or her from an extremely painful or slow agonizing death when there is no hope for recovery. Nearly everyone at some time faces the question of how to care for a dying person. We may face it with grandparents, parents, spouses, ourselves, and most tragically, with children. Life presses us with the need to understand our own assessment of death and dying as well as that of our loved ones. This chapter attempts to clarify some of the facts surrounding euthanasia as well as offering ethical considerations to guide us in preparing for eventual heart-rending decisions.

Before examining the ethical issues, several important distinctions must be clarified. The distinction between active and passive euthanasia stands out as the most important. Active euthanasia means performing an act that directly causes the death of the person. This would almost always consist of a lethal injection given with the intention of killing the patient. Passive euthanasia, often called "letting die" rather than "killing," means withholding or ceasing treatment that keeps a person alive and allowing him or her to die naturally. To avoid a common confusion, passive euthanasia does not necessarily mean "doing nothing." It might involve an act performed by a medical-professional such as removing a ventilator or feeding tube. The death results from the disease or accident, not from the medical procedure.

The ethical questions concerning euthanasia center on the duty toward a dying person who has no hope of recovery and whose death involves severe pain and suffering. The three central questions are: When is it permissible to withdraw or withhold treatment thereby allowing the patient to die? Is it ever permissible to practice active euthanasia? Is the distinction between active and passive euthanasia pertinent?

The Traditional Ethical Position and the Current Legal Standing

The present legal position, one that is supported by the medical profession as well as by the Catholic Church, is expressed in a Statement adopted by the House of Delegates of the American Medical Association, December 4, 1973.

> The intentional termination of the life of one human being by another—mercy killing—is contrary to that for which the medical profession stands and is contrary to the policy of the American Medical Association.
>
> The cessation of the employment of extraordinary means to prolong the life of the body when there is irrefutable evidence that biological death is imminent is the decision of the patient and/or his immediate family. The advice and judgment of the physician should be freely available to the patient and/or his immediate family.[134]

This statement embodies two premises, each of which requires clarification. The first premise affirms that it is always wrong to deliberately kill an innocent person; the second premise allows that under certain circumstances the duty to prolong life does not apply. In short, the statement rejects active euthanasia, but permits passive euthanasia under certain circumstances.

The first premise forbids directly and intentionally killing an innocent person. The AMA statement represents the professional ethics of medicine, an ethical position supported by law and by most religious thought and authority. The medical profession upholds the principle of preserving and sustaining human life. Although mortality hovers as a defining condition of human life, medical personnel are educated and dedicated to preventing unnecessary and premature death. The notion of intervening in a way to hasten or bring about death runs contrary to the motivating ideal of the profession.

Euthanasia constitutes one of the social-ethical issues that focus on exceptions to the ethical and legal ban against killing human beings. Other issues that examine this exception include abortion, capital punishment, and war. Active euthanasia represents an illegal act that some hold as ethically right and contend that under certain circumstances should be legal. Those who oppose active euthanasia often do so because they hold human life sacred and of such supreme value that it should never be deliberately destroyed. This core belief usually entails an opposition to war and capital punishment, and in many cases, to abortion. The view of life as sacred upholds the prohibition against killing as absolute and fundamental; it depends on no contingent circumstance and needs no justification. Any argument for euthanasia must reject the absoluteness of this prohibition.

Before considering the more controversial case for active euthanasia, we will clarify the conditions for allowing passive euthanasia. Ordinarily, human beings have the obligation, not only to refrain from killing other humans but also to prevent them from dying whenever possible. By analogy, if a child or any person were drowning in shallow water, we would be obligated to save them, even if we had not caused them to be in the water.

For medical professionals the duty to save lives stands out as an explicit duty. But the AMA statement allows for the cessation of extraordinary means to prolong life "when there is indisputable evidence that death is imminent." The patient in this case has no hope of recovery and has no future except dying and death.

Distinguishing ordinary and extraordinary measures does not always come easily. Extraordinary measures, sometimes called heroic measures, are those that are not ordinarily performed because of the negative impact on the patient, for example, amputation of a limb.

Others that may be considered heroic are mechanical respiration, cardiopulmonary resuscitation, and artificial hydration and nutrition. Under some circumstances it is permissible to withhold extraordinary means of keeping a person alive thereby allowing the person to die. Treatments that usually are considered "ordinary" such as antibiotics may in some cases be omitted as extraordinary in that they offer no benefit to the patient.

These circumstances are limited to those in which the patient suffers a terminal disease with no hope of recovery. Patients who have a degree of lucidity to make the decision themselves obviously have that right. For patients who cannot speak for themselves, decision-makers must ask whether forestalling death benefits the dying person. If the person has no hope of meaningful thoughts and communication with others, then the patient has no future, no unfulfilled potential. If the person has any feeling, the extraordinary procedures may cause nothing but pain and emotional distress. The best ethical choice may be to allow the most peaceful death possible under the circumstances.

Opposition to the Traditional Position

Philosopher James Rachels offers an argument against the traditional position.[135]

Rachels argues that the distinction between active and passive euthanasia is untenable logically and wrong ethically. He cites the case of a baby born with Down's syndrome who has an intestinal obstruction that requires surgery. Without surgery, the baby cannot take any food or water and will die of dehydration over a period of days. The surgery is not prohibitively difficult, and if the baby did not have Down's syndrome, there would be no hesitation to perform the surgery. Rachels argues that the baby should have been saved, (and most people agree). But he argues further, that if the baby were permitted to die, it should have been given a lethal injection rather than being allowed to die slowly of hunger and dehydration.

Rachels contends that the distinction between active and passive euthanasia is irrelevant because whether we allow the baby to starve or give it a lethal injection, we intend and cause the death of the baby. The two methods differ only in that the injection saves the baby pain and saves the hospital staff the anguish of watching a baby starve to death.

Those who defend the traditional position agree with Rachels that the baby should not have been allowed to die. The surgery did not constitute "extraordinary" means because there would have been no hesitation to perform the surgery if the child had been otherwise healthy. The refusal stemmed from the fact that the baby had Down's syndrome and its death constituted the intentional and inevitable outcome of the refusal.

The traditional distinction stands on the principle that while we cannot rightly perform an act with the intention of killing an innocent person, we may refrain from actions that cause the patient harm out of proportion to the benefit of postponing their death. The ethical theory that traditionally supports this distinction is the principle of double effect. According to the principle we may rightly perform an act that intends a good effect, even if there are foreseeable but unavoidable and undesirable effects that follow. This justification holds true only if the undesirable effects are not disproportionate to the good effects. In the case of passive euthanasia, we withhold extraordinary means of keeping a person alive to spare the person the suffering that the procedures would cause. Hastening the death is a foreseeable but unintended result.

Because the advance in medical technology continually blurs the distinction between the ordinary and extraordinary, we cannot always draw a line to determine what constitutes extraordinary. Unfortunately for people who desire clear and distinct answers to ethical questions, ambiguities continue to abound. For example, we may remove a loved one from a ventilator without the intention of killing him or her. If the patient breathes on his own, he lives a while longer. By contrast when we remove a feeding tube from a patient who cannot take nourishment any other way, that person will inevitably starve to death. Perhaps we need to rephrase the question. Instead of asking whether we are intending the death of the person, we should ask whether the procedure is really saving the person's life or merely prolonging his or her death.

A deeper more fundamental question challenges the traditional ban on intentional killing. Rachels, for one, argues that active euthanasia stands as a moral equivalent to passive euthanasia. He argues that when a patient has reached a point where death constitutes the best option for that individual, and the person, when lucid, had clearly expressed a desire for euthanasia under clearly stated circumstances, then active euthanasia emerges as the best ethical option. Opponents might question whether the circumstances can ever be clear enough, but in fact they could be the very same circumstances that would permit withholding or removing extraordinary life-saving procedures.[136]

Reverence for Relations with those who are Dying

The argument against active euthanasia stands on the premise that intentionally bringing about the death of an innocent person constitutes a morally bad action. But a deeper question asks why we disapprove of killing. In the argument against abortion presented in the previous chapter, Don Marquis argues that the wrongfulness of killing stems from the fact that we deprive a person of his or her future. This argument pertains to humans who have not yet had a chance to live and have all of their potential ahead of them. Marquis explicitly states that his argument does not apply to those who are at the end of their lives. Since death is a natural part of life, we need to ask if death at some point becomes the best hope of the dying person. We can best approach this question by asking whether, when a person approaches the end of life, death remains a bad outcome.

Death is bad when it deprives a person of his or her future, even if the future consists of a relatively short time period. Does the person have something to look forward to, such as a visit from a loved one or the birth of a grandchild? At some point the future becomes empty in that there is nothing that the person looks forward to, or it becomes closed in that the person can no longer experience it. Philosopher Tom Morris provided an elegant definition of the meaning of life as "loving creativity or creative loving."[137] At some point a person has no remaining potential for loving or creativity. Life-prolonging procedures no longer benefit such a person and death may become a good outcome.

Death becomes good when a person has reached the final stages of a terminal illness with no hope of recovery. Nothing awaits him except dying and death. The only thing he can experience, if anything at all, is suffering and dying. When our loved ones reach that state, we have no qualms wishing and even praying for their passing. Does it follow that when death constitutes the person's best outcome, that for which those who love her hope for, that we ought to act on our wishes and hasten death by active euthanasia? This argument has some support although there are strong social arguments opposing it. One opposing argument consists of the "slippery slope." The argument contends that once we have crossed the line of permitting active euthanasia, there may be a tendency to adopt it more and more quickly. This holds especially true in an age in which our public and private health care insurers and our medical facilities are under financial distress and ending a person's life might appear to be good for society before it is good for the individual. An "uncluttering" mentality would not only lead to disrespect for life, but greatly increase the sense of despair and alienation of those who feel targeted.

Another, more personal argument stands against active euthanasia. Active euthanasia deprives the dying person from experiencing whatever stage of growth the dying process might entail. Elizabeth Kubler-Ross, who studied death and dying as intimately as anyone ever has, called death the final stage of growth.[138] Opponents of this position may argue against it reasonably on the grounds that we do not know for sure what dying is like, and perhaps it does not involve any experience at all, especially for those who are comatose. But while a Socratic humility, admitting that we do not know, makes the most sense, the benefit of doubt favors allowing the person the opportunity of the death experience if there be such. The possibility of such an experience may also apply to people who can no longer communicate to the outside world. Of course, as Scott Peck argued, extreme pain would destroy any possibility of a good death and so patients should not be deprived of pain medication, even if the medication hastens death.[139] For those who hold the hypothesis that a person ought to be allowed the chance to experience death, it follows those procedures that futilely postpone death, procedures such as feeding tubes, would also interfere with natural dying, and so permission to remove them should be granted. In summary, we should not kill dying people, but when there is no longer hope of recovery, we should allow them the most peaceful death possible.

1. What is desirable as opposed to merely desired?

2. How can you best enhance your personal integrity as well as that of other persons, and

  your integration with each other?

3. How would you treat each person in the situation if you felt positive respect and

  affection for them?

4. How may we use moral imagination in this situation to nourish the good of

teleological harmony?

CHAPTER 10
Punishment and the Death Penalty

The reality of crime constitutes a failure of society to achieve a true teleological harmony or integration. The reality is that some individuals, for whatever reason, do not choose to abide by the agreed upon laws of society. We need to face the problem of dealing with criminals in a way that maintains our loyalty to a just society, and that respects all of the relations of life, including the relation of society to convicted criminals.

Justification of Punishment: Four Reasons

Dealing with criminals poses one of the greatest challenges to any society that hopes to live by ethical standards. A society based on unbridled power with no countervailing ethical standards can dispose of criminals at the pleasure of those who wield the power. But if we strive to act ethically in our criminal justice system, we face problems that we do not ordinarily face dealing with each other. When we as a society punish criminals, we do things to them that would be wrong if done to an innocent person. Punishment of lawbreakers consists of taking a portion of their wealth in fines, depriving them of liberty for a period of time or even for life, or killing them by capital punishment. Ethics generally requires us to do good to all people, but punishment clearly does harm. The assertion that punishment harms criminals does not imply that the punishment is ethically wrong, but punishment poses serious practical and theoretical questions for any ethics. Those who work in law enforcement, the courts, and the prison system face problems that most of us do not experience. But we cannot avoid our moral responsibility for understanding what constitutes right and wrong in forming policy and in the carrying out of such policy. Each of us, as citizens, has the duty to examine the purposes and the results of the practices of our criminal justice system.

Ethicists give four reasons to justify punishment of criminals: *prevention, deterrence, retribution and revenge, and rehabilitation.* The list includes five reasons if revenge and retribution are treated separately. The connotation of the terms is somewhat different, but because they are so closely related and entwined, I will deal with them as a single, though complicated, principle. These four (or five) reasons do not mutually exclude each other and, in principle, all of the reasons could be integrated.

The whole criminal justice system, from the police officers on the streets to the prisons, serve to *protect* the rest of society from crime. The most obvious type of protection consists of confining a person who has committed a crime so that, for at least a period of time, the convicted person does not have access to the general population. Capital punishment obviously prevents the person from any further crime.

Deterrence refers to using the threat of punishment to provide a negative incentive to those who might otherwise commit a crime. The effectiveness of deterrence is hard to measure since would-be criminals do not, as a rule, report that they were deterred from a crime. In fact, the person who refrains from crime only because of a deterring punishment might not even be aware of it. People, even those who live in high-crime areas, do not ordinarily break store windows to steal items. But in times of civil turmoil, many citizens, who see other people looting with no apparent consequences, might join in and help themselves to whatever they find available. A more common example of the power of deterrence shows up when ordinary citizens, driving on roads that they believe are not patrolled, violate the speed limit with no qualms. Former House Speaker Newt Gingrich once extolled such contempt for law as a positive aspect of the American character. These same citizens become very observant of the law when they see a marked police car or receive a warning on their radar detectors.

Revenge and retribution constitute an entirely different reason for punishment. If a person does something bad, then, the thinking goes, something bad should happen to that person. This is a human tendency that some ethicists consider to be irrational. Christianity also considers the desire for revenge as a temptation to which we should not yield. And yet, St. Augustine argued that there must be punishment after life for sinners, because it would be an imbalance if some people could do serious wrong and suffer no consequences.

Retribution means that a criminal should pay the victim for the damages that the criminal has caused. In the case of theft or vandalism, the wrong-doer may be forced to pay the victim. Sometimes a convicted person is assigned "community service" to repay society for a crime. The term retribution is often used in place of revenge. For example, some refer to prison time as "paying a debt to society." Prison inmates, of course, are not paying anything back and their incarceration becomes a further financial burden on the society that they have injured.

Rehabilitation refers to the notion that the punishment will teach the person to live a crime-free life in the way that "drug rehab" is meant to enable the person to live drug-free. Rehabilitation sounds like a good idea, but suffers many fatal flaws. Our criminal justice system does not have an acceptable record when it comes to rehabilitation. Prisons do not have the resources and do not even claim to rehabilitate. Even in cases in which rehabilitation is the explicit goal, the success rate has been dismal. For example, many sex offenders, who were supposedly rehabilitated, committed the crime again.

Even if rehabilitation were reasonably successful, it would pose problems. If there is a legitimate need for retribution, rehabilitation does not meet the need. Granted that those who believe the goal of criminal justice should be rehabilitation do not accept the legitimacy of retribution, yet there is strong sentiment for retribution, and the rehabilitationists are not likely to win this battle any time soon.

But desire for revenge is not the only moral argument against rehabilitation. Those who hold that ethics consists essentially of respecting all human beings as rational and responsible,[140] point out that rehabilitation treats the criminal as a problem to be fixed rather than as a person who freely chose an outlawed act. While rehabilitation seems benign, it denies free will, at least implicitly, and does not respect the person as a moral being who chooses his act and the consequences of that act. Teaching a person a trade or otherwise helping him or her find a way to earn a living constitutes a good action whether the person has broken the law or not. But such assistance should not be identified with punishment.

Commonly Cited Ethical Theories

Ethicists who debate this issue generally argue from one of two basic standpoints. While such labeling is almost always simplistic and slips into false generalizations, the classification into utilitarian and deontological (an ethics based on duty) can be useful as an initial approach to understanding the diversity of viewpoints. But like all such generalizations, these should be accompanied by a healthy critical attitude and the desire to look for more nuanced distinctions. With the above disclaimer in mind, we will look first at the utilitarian rationale for punishment and then at the deontological.

Utilitarians argue for maximizing good, which they understand as happiness. Those who follow the philosophy of John Stuart Mill, the author of *Utilitarianism* and creator of the term, are concerned not only with the majority, "the greatest number," but with every individual affected by an action or a practice. Utilitarians base their theories of punishment on prevention, deterrence, and rehabilitation. Revenge is generally rejected as irrational, although Mill himself thought it played a genuine role in relieving the anguish and anger of victims. Most utilitarians oppose capital punishment, although their theory does not rule it out.

Ethicists in the tradition of Immanuel Kant, who reject the utilitarian ethics, argue that we should act respectfully toward each person regardless of the outcome. To respect a person means to treat him or her as an "end" and not merely as a means to an end. To treat persons as "ends" means to acknowledge that they exist for their own sake, and not merely as tools to accomplish some external purpose. These ethicists, called deontologists from the Greek word for duty, contend that rehabilitation does not respect persons as autonomous, and therefore responsible for their actions and the consequences of those actions. Rather, they contend, rehabilitation treats them as things that society can fix and manipulate to its own ends.

Deontologists also reject deterrence because it makes the criminal a means to the end of intimidating other would-be criminals. Retribution, by contrast, respects criminals by allowing them to reap the results of their own choice. When a person chooses to commit a crime, that person is choosing the penalties that result from being caught.

We as a society and especially those responsible for making policy do not need to be pure utilitarians or deontologists. The task of policy-makers consists of finding the best solution to a bad situation, namely, that some people commit crimes. The variety of crimes and criminals may be too big to be contained by any one theory. But we can follow the general rule that a good policy protects citizens while being fair to the criminals. One way of judging fairness to criminals, is to agree that if we, or someone we love, committed a crime, we would want them to be treated the way we want all criminals to be treated.

The Death Penalty

Rehabilitation is generally not given as a reason for capital punishment. When we execute a person, we have effectively given up on him or her as a member of the human community. Of course, we may believe that the proximity of death can lead to repentance and motivate the person to make peace with God. But such theological speculations do not enter into the deliberations of our judicial system, nor should they.

Arguments for the death penalty most often center on the effectiveness of deterrence and the moral validity of revenge. Weak arguments often arise such as "Why should we let a murderer live and support him for his whole life with tax-payer money?" Aside from the fact that keeping a death row and facilities for execution is more expensive than "feeding the person,"[141] we would certainly degrade ourselves as a society if we made life and death decisions based on cutting the cost of feeding a prisoner. So, revenge and deterrence stand as the serious arguments for the death penalty.

If revenge is legitimate, then the death penalty would be justified for the crime of murder. The term revenge has a mean-spirited sound to it, and so those who want to kill a murderer to even the score probably prefer the term retribution. So, I will use "retribution" to avoid slanting the argument. The overriding question is what should happen to persons who commit an extremely evil act such as cold-blooded murder, mass murder, or murder of a child? Is it all right for them to live a happy life with no bad consequences to themselves? Those who answer the last question negatively—the vast majority of us––must assume some validity for retribution whether or not we condone the death penalty.

Opponents of the death penalty argue that a life in prison with no chance of parole is sufficient. The proponents of the death penalty argue that for heinous crimes nothing short of death suffices. Such people are disturbed by the very thought of the murderer living in prison while his or her victims lie dead and their families endure a never-ending loss. Those who favor the death penalty contend that the prohibition against killing is not absolute and they consider retribution as legitimate.

Although retribution makes little sense in utilitarian terms, it does seem to coincide with our instinctive notion that justice requires a punishment proportionate to the crime. Opponents sometimes try to laugh this argument out of court by pointing out that nobody advocates raping rapists or burning down the houses of arsonists. And some crimes, such a mass murders, are so appalling that no punishment can match the crime. But those who advocate the death penalty maintain that those who have crossed a line by showing a lack of respect for the life of another have forfeited their own right to life and should suffer the ultimate penalty.

Deterrence serves as foundation for some advocates of the death penalty. Perhaps the strongest such argument came from Ernest van den Haag, former law professor at Fordham.[142] He argues that while we cannot gather statistics on how many murderers are deterred by the death penalty, there are compelling reasons to affirm that it does deter. While some criminals, such as suicide bombers want to die, most human beings including criminals yearn to stay alive. Therefore, the threat of a death penalty will almost certainly deter some crimes. The argument for deterrence must convince us only that the death penalty deters some murders, not that it can deter all of them. For instance, a person planning to rob a convenience grocery store may be willing to take a chance on going to prison, but not risk being executed. Therefore, in committing his crime he may avoid using a loaded gun, or at least be careful not to fire it. One such incident means that the life of a store clerk is saved. So, if the death penalty deters murder, it is reasonable to assume that the law saves the life of many such store clerks and other potential victims. If this assumption holds true, then the abolition of capital punishment unintentionally leads to the death of those whose lives could have been saved. This argument bears a lot of weight and puts the burden of proof on those who oppose capital punishment.

Many opponents of the death penalty base their argument on the wrongness of deliberately killing any person and hold that the prohibition against killing is absolute. Those who affirm the absolute value of all human life also oppose abortion, active euthanasia, and war. Focusing here on the issue of capital punishment, the principle of universal non-violence may be reasonably asserted, but defending it proves to be difficult.

The most crucial ethical question on the issue of capital punishment consists of whether we hold the value of human life as unconditional. Maintaining the premise of the unconditional value of human life requires the conclusion that no person can forfeit life, even by a crime in which he or she rejects the value of life. Further, we could not execute murderers to deter others, even if such deterrence yields a significant benefit. Giving up the deterrent value of capital punishment constitutes the highest price for upholding the unconditional worth of human life.

Affirming the value of life as described above would not necessarily imply absolute non-violence although non-violence stands out as the most consistent consequence of this value. A person may hold that life is unconditionally valuable and still justify killing in self-defense or in defense of an innocent person, for example, a police officer shooting a gunman. The intention of such defensive killing is saving a life when killing another is the only means available. This interpretation would make a just war possible, at least in theory. A person who holds a strong pro-life position regarding the unborn could justify abortion to save the life of the mother. In summary, the value of human life would exclude all unnecessary killing of human beings. Killing a human being can be called "necessary" only when such killing constitutes the only way to save an innocent human life.

Moral Evolution

Capital punishment has been around for a long time and its advocates can find justification for it in our religious and political traditions. The scriptures of Judaism, Christianity, and Islam condone capital punishment. The framers of the Bill of Rights, which excludes "cruel and unusual punishment," did not outlaw the death penalty.

On the other hand, morality evolves. For example, the Scriptures and the Founding Fathers allowed both slavery and wars that we would deem as genocidal. Regarding capital punishment, Justices Brennan and Marshall argued that as social norms develop, the notion of what constitutes cruel and unusual punishment can change. [143]

While I will argue that we ought to move toward the abolishment of capital punishment, I will not attempt to prove that the advocates are wrong. Advocates of capital punishment might be right in asserting that it deters some murders and that it fulfills a natural need for retribution. Throughout this book, I have attempted to make the case that ethics has a larger task than merely determining which actions are wrong and hence should be avoided. Ethics must also nourish the good. The ethical theory that defines good as "teleological harmony," or purposive integration, indicates that we should move toward creating a society that rejects all killing and hence opposes the death penalty.

To frame the issue in a larger historical context, the whole moral evolution of the human race tends toward an ever-increasing respect for human life. This statement may sound ludicrous in an era that outdoes all others in massive and genocidal murders. And yet these crimes do not necessarily refute the notion of moral progress. Moral evolution, like biological evolution, does not always move in a straight line. Crimes against humanity can constitute aberrations. Their gruesome effectiveness results from modern technology that produces killing tools, from lethal gases to automatic weapons to the motorized mobility of the murderers. But although "The World," in the person of national political, religious, and cultural leaders, has often been too slow in condemning and preventing mass murders, it does ultimately and inexorably move in that direction. From the beginning of history, "other people" were looked on as an enemy to be killed or as a resource to be enslaved. Even those nations that were at the forefront of our civilization, the Hebrews and the Greeks, had no compunction in killing Philistines and barbarians, respectively. The history of the United States is marred by crimes against Blacks and American Indians. But today, we are no more likely to hear an American political leader defend slavery or genocidal war against the native population, than you are to hear a German leader defend the Holocaust.

The above paragraph may have sounded like a digression. But the point is that morals––/ personal and societal––are moving, all too slowly, toward a greater respect for life. Fewer nations have the death penalty today than did one hundred years ago. In the United States, fewer crimes result in the death penalty, and fewer states have a death penalty.

While I do not look on advocates of the death penalty as unethical—they have some strong arguments as I cited above—my thesis is that we are evolving toward a respect for life based on universal human solidarity. Those who commit murder are guilty of the most egregious violation and ought to be imprisoned for the rest of their lives. But the message we send to all of our citizens especially our youth, is that killing is not an option, and our society, as represented by our laws, is much better than those who commit crimes against us, and that we never stoop to killing.

CHAPTER 11
Loyalty and Reverence for Relationship as a Universal Ethical Standard

Teleological Harmony

This work, inspired primarily by Josiah Royce, presents a vision of ethical living that can lead the reader beyond the right vs. wrong concepts of most ethics books. This view does not deny that some things are right and others wrong, but affirms that ethics requires us to grow beyond that mere dichotomy. A vision of the *good* can inspire and instruct us on how to choose right actions and avoid wrong ones. Right actions nourish the *good*; wrong actions starve or impede its growth. For Royce, the meaning of the *good* consists of "teleological harmony" meaning that the ethical purpose of our acts provides integration of our individual and communal lives. Royce emphasized *autonomy* and *duty* as the parts of the triad, which along with the *good*, constitute the vision that ethics serves. *Autonomy* expresses the uniqueness and freedom of the individual in making choices. *Duty* expresses the connections with others, individually and collectively, that guide the autonomous person in choosing what is *good*. The view of Royce allows us to avoid the ideological blindness that comes from false dichotomies such as egoism vs. altruism, or individualism vs. collectivism. A person cannot become a healthy well-developed individual without serving a social cause, nor can the person serve a social cause without becoming a healthy, strong, and autonomous individual. This concluding chapter looks at the central principles that govern the relationship of the individual and society and follows up by explicitly connecting them to the issues that were discussed in the earlier chapters.

Three central themes stand out in the ethical vision of Josiah Royce, themes that hopefully have animated the present text: *loyalty, reverence for relationships, and teleological harmony.* These three fit together to compose an ethics that defines right and wrong as well as better and worse, in terms of what best nourishes the *good.* After a brief description of each of Royce's three themes, this concluding chapter will illustrate how these themes guide ethical action in the areas discussed in chapters three through nine.

Royce offered as a preliminary definition of loyalty: "the practical and thorough-going devotion to a cause."[144] This definition gave us an instrument for examining the issues presented in the earlier chapters. Royce understands a *cause* as some purpose that is larger than the individual and that involves cooperation with other individuals. Loyalty enables the person to overcome "the shadow of the ego." However, there is a danger that those devoted to a cause may slip into "collective narcissism."[145] Examples of such collective narcissism range from a street gang, to a drug cartel, to a fundamentalist religious sect, to an imperialistic nation. Such loyalty can be extremely dangerous and destructive.

Royce's answer to the problem is what he calls "loyalty to loyalty."[146] Since every person needs some cause to overcome the despair of egoism, destroying a person's loyalty is the worst thing you can do to any person, and fostering loyalty is the best thing. Loyalty to loyalty means that you serve your own cause and also respect and even foster the cause of another, except to the extent that the other's cause is destructive.

In the final chapter of *Philosophy of Loyalty,* "Loyalty and Religion," Royce's offers a more highly developed definition. *"Loyalty is the will to believe in something eternal and to express that belief in the practical life of a human being"* (Italics in original).[147] Royce argues that loyalty is religious as well as moral. He does not limit his use of the term "religious" to the ordinary sense of faith traditions and communities, which he calls "the visible church." Instead, he offers a wider notion of religion that embraces many who do not consider themselves religious. Royce addresses the loyal person:

> Through your loyalty, you, then, know yourself to be kin to all the loyal. You hereupon conceive the loyal as one brotherhood, one invisible church, for which and in which you live. The spirit dwells within this invisible church––the holy spirit that wills the unity of all in fidelity and in service. [148]

Royce affirms that religion in his sense depends on two assertions; first, "That there is some one highest end of existence, some goal of life, some chief good," and second, "That by nature, man is in great danger of completely failing to attain this good, so that he needs to be saved from this danger."[149] Religions, such as Christianity and Buddhism, obviously show this structure in which we need to be saved from sin or from wrong-mindedness. But persons who do not adhere to a traditional religion but believe that there is a highest good such as scientific progress, artistic creativity, social justice, or individual flourishing, also fit Royce's of definition of religion.

Loyalty includes morality and religion. The moral aspect consists in the need to choose a cause and to actively work in its service. Repeating his preliminary definition, Loyalty is "the willing, practical, thorough-going devotion of a self to a cause." [150] The religious aspect of the cause consists in its being revealed as a gift, a grace. The revelation may come in the form of something "human, dear, and vitally fascinating." For example, it may come in the form of a human face or a living community. Describing the effect of this revelation Royce says:

The cause is a religious object. It finds you in your need. It points out to you the way of salvation. Its presence in your world is to you a free gift from the realm of the spirit––a gift that you have not of yourself but through the willingness of the world to manifest to you the way of salvation. This free gift at first compels your love. Then you freely give yourself in return. [151]

While a person reading this quotation out of context might say that it could describe a cult, the context of Royce's "loyalty to loyalty" as described in Chapter One makes it clear that the loyal person respects the loyalty of everyone's cause, except the cause that destroys the cause of others. Royce reminds the reader that whatever a person's special cause is, *"your true cause is the spiritual unity of all the world of reasonable beings"* (Italics in the original).[152] The cause must be specific and personal to allow for practical thorough-going devotion. But the cause takes its legitimacy and full meaning by advancing the cause of universal loyalty.

Reverence for Relations

In order for individuals and communities to be healthy, individuals must respect and revere not only themselves and their neighbors as individuals, but also the relationships that tie them together. The clearest example is a marriage in which the man and woman not only love and revere each other, but also have a strong loyalty to the marriage itself. Such reverence enables them to get through rough times when one or both of them become unlovable. Similarly, a group of friends must revere the friendship as well as each other.[153] This notion applies to workplaces, professions, communities, churches, and nations.

The classical philosophers, especially St. Thomas Aquinas, acknowledged that being is good. This is a tenet not only of Catholics, but all Christians, Jews and others who believe that there is one Creator. Many non-religious secular humanists can also affirm the goodness of being through experience.[154] Evil consists of the absence or deficiency of being.

Evolutionary science gives us a greater insight into the very meaning of *being* and what it means to affirm the goodness of being. *The being of all of nature consists of becoming.* Natural entities, which St. Thomas called "created entities," achieve their being, and therefore their goodness, over time. Describing this development in terms of our contemporary biology, organisms develop by cells and tissues becoming ever more specialized and integrated. At a higher level, the life story of any person who grows successfully to emotional and spiritual maturity consists in that person's passions, desires, thoughts, dreams and goals being integrated around a life-plan to serve a cause. A healthy society is one in which the individuals who compose it grow in respect for each other, and in respect for the society itself, and become integrated in the pursuit of their individual and collective purposes. Good may be defined as "purposive integration." Good actions have the purpose of bringing about integrity and integration; evil actions impede or attack this goal.

Individual Relations

Royce argued that a relation between two individuals always requires a third entity to serve as mediator. Pairs can be dangerous in their competition and hostility toward each other. One person may come to dominate the other thus inhibiting that person's growth, or the two may fall apart into enmity. Shakespeare's Petronius warned "Neither a borrower nor a lender be." This is good advice because failure to repay a loan in a timely fashion can destroy friendship. However, a third person, a banker, can borrow from Peter and lend to Paul without any animosity between Peter and Paul. Acting as a third party is often the task of police officers, courts, insurance companies, and, of course, sports officials. In a personal friendship, there need not be a third individual between two friends, but a long-lasting friendship requires loyalty to a third principle such as the friendship itself. People often build friendships around a third principle of loyalty such as a military unit, college days, sports and other activities, work experience, the old neighborhood, or their children's school activities.

But even if we can pare friendship down to two persons who simply like each other, there is still a three-way dynamic. Each person acts as an interpreter to the other. One person might be the interpreter and the one interpreted. This may seem hopelessly abstract, but a simple example can bring it to earth. A mentor sees some potential in a student, a potential of which the student is unaware. The mentor interprets the student to him or herself. Or the mentor shares a personal insight with the student. Now the mentor is interpreting himself to the student. The same dynamic occurs in a friendship between equals. Aristotle described the best friendship as one in which the two persons see the good in each other. We can understand the essence of the relationship in constantly developing this awareness through mutual interpretation. Such a dynamic requires loyalty and reverence for the relationship and leads to an integration of the two individuals that enhances each of them.

Erotic Relations

The chapter on friendship interpreted erotic relationship as a special kind of friendship that involves sexual desire for and appreciation of physical beauty in the loved one. Mere sexual desire can instigate behavior that is immoral and even criminal as in the cases of sexual assault or sex with a minor. A relationship of two consenting adults based on sexual desire alone may consist of one using the other or both using each other. The mutuality would make the using fairer, but hardly commendable. More sinisterly, the relation may be one of dominance or a battle for dominance. Such relationships are not likely to have a good outcome and occasionally lead to tragically violent endings. Also, when we hear of public figures engaging in the kind of sexual activity that involves only some combination of lust and the will to power, it does not inspire our admiration for them, and it is seldom a part of their life of which they admit to being proud.

We can call an erotic relationship "good" in every sense of the word when the lovers share devotion, not only to each other, but to the relationship itself. The joy, thrill, and fun of "falling in love" cannot last forever, but the memory of it can. The erotic relationship can be one of the best glimpses we have of what human harmony can be. But the commitment of two persons to each other that outlives the youthful exuberance can best be described by Royce's concept of loyalty, the thorough-going and practical devotion to a cause. In this case the cause is the commitment of the persons to each other. In many cases the benefits of the commitment are shared by others, especially children and grandchildren but also friends and family. Of course, sometimes the most committed relationships break down. But such is the tragedy of human existence in that people need loyal relationships but find them to be extremely difficult to sustain.

Business Relations

Chapter three applied the concepts of loyalty and reverence for relations to business ethics. For business to be ethical, and for business to be efficient and effective, the participants must act with loyalty, not only to their own business or the business that they work for, but also to the whole business community. Relationships include manager to employee, manager to investors and creditors, producers to consumers, vendors to buyers, and firms to local communities, firms to competitors, professionals such as accountants and engineers to their professions. Tom Morris, author of *If Aristotle Ran General Motors,* offers a powerful definition of the ethical relationship between autonomous individuals performing their duty to build a healthy community: "Ethics is all about: **spiritually healthy people in socially harmonious relationships**" [155] (Bold in the original). This expression merges perfectly with Royce's notion of the good. Spirituality consists of inner depth, which enables persons to perceive a fuller meaning in their life and work and to make ever larger connections with the people and world around them. Harmonious relationships foster the growth of each person and empower them to achieve their own highest potential while enhancing the common enterprise.

Therefore, in an ethical business environment, each person understands the work, the product, and the relationship of all who contribute to its production. They further see how the product contributes to the overall good of the society in which the business flourishes. This description of an ethical business environment may sound unrealistic and would be unrealistic if it presupposed perfect human beings in idyllic settings. But an analogy to physical health might provide some clarity.

A common structure may be found in physical, mental, organizational and spiritual health. We call ourselves *physically healthy* when all of our systems are functioning so that we feel good and have a high level of strength and energy. Our whole body maintains balance. For example, our immune system protects us from infectious disease without overacting and causing auto-immune disease. The term harmony describes the state of health well, and Plato compared a healthy body to a well-tuned instrument.

Mental health includes the ability to see the world without distortion and to face the challenges of life with a realistic confidence. Mental illness, in varying degrees, may limit a person to a narrow perception of reality, make concentration difficult if not impossible, and it may cause things to be seen as disconnected and chaotic. This is not, of course, a complete description of all mental illness,[156] but these features certainly show a diminished state of mental health. Royce's definition of reasonableness coincides with mental health. Royce defines reason as "...the power to see widely, steadily and connectedly."[157] As with physical and mental health, a *healthy organization* fulfills its function effectively in a way that promotes the growth and health of its members, their ability to work in cooperation, and contributes to the well-being of the larger society.

Spiritual health goes deeper and provides the healthy person with insight into the worth of every individual as at least potential members of the community and appreciates the worth of the community itself. Royce's understanding of loyalty expresses the meaning of spiritual health. As Frank Oppenheim describes genuine loyalty:

> Its distinctive point is the will to love and serve the universal community *as* community. This loyalty leads to the universal community of all minded selves and thus to the felt presence of the divine. It may not exclude any self insofar as that self is or may become universally loyal.[158]

Few people are perfectly healthy in a physical sense; some are morbidly ill; most of us lie somewhere between. But each of us, as well as our doctors and other health care professionals, has the need to know what "healthy" means and how to strive toward it. Rather than thinking of health as all or nothing—we are perfect specimens or we are dying—we think of ourselves as more or less healthy and can adopt habits to become more so, or at least stave off becoming less so. The range of healthiness applies also to mental and spiritual health.

The notion of health and sickness applies to our business life. The terms teleological and purposive, as used throughout this book, have emphasized that the good is a goal, a task to be achieved, not a ready-made characteristic. Those who desire to work ethically must be sure that the business in which they work is not hopelessly unethical because of a harmful product, a dishonorable way of doing business, or toxic relationships within the business. When ethical persons have chosen a business in which they believe they can work, they strive to the best of their ability to work loyally toward more harmonious relationships that contribute positively to all who are affected.

The Natural Environment

Living ethically requires loyalty to the web of life that sustains us. For the religious believer, reverence for the Creator, if it were properly understood, would lead to respect for creation as it emerges through the evolutionary process. Those who cannot believe in the notion of a Creator can still experience a sense of reverence perhaps based on a pantheistic spirituality. But whatever theological assumptions or lack thereof guide people, they can still experience reverence for the web of natural relationships from which our life has emerged and which sustains us. The object of loyalty in this case is the whole biosphere to which some people devote their entire lives. Those devoted to the biosphere include most obviously, environmental scientists, but also writers, educators, poets, artists, philosophers, and theologians and others who make the rest of us aware of the deep dependence and connectedness that we have to the physical environment. We need to experience the natural world not merely on an intellectual level, but also on a deeper aesthetic and emotional level. Most of the population may have some other cause as the chief claim to their loyalty, but all of us need to actively affirm environmental health in our private lives and in the public policies that we support.

Birth and Death

Two of the most controversial issues in contemporary society center on how our loyalty to life extends to those not yet born and those near death. Since we do not have a consensus as to whether the unborn are members of the human community, I agree, somewhat reluctantly, that the question ought not to be answered by the state but rather by the woman who bears the pre-natal life. But moral awareness and reverence for relationships ought to extend to all living humans including the unborn. This cannot be achieved by trying to make abortion illegal, but by creating conditions that favor choosing life.

Currently our political ideologies spew out a tangle of contradictory notions that lead to an appalling deficit of reverence for life and the relationships that sustain life. Liberals sometimes seem to have little or no concern for life before birth; conservatives who parade under the "pro-life" banner often care little for poor children once they are born. Many, who would ban abortion, simultaneously strive to block policies that would assure that all pregnant women have access to pre-natal, post-natal and pediatric care. Besides medical care, a child needs a decent place to live and an education that empowers him or her to be self-reliant, law-abiding and able to contribute to the community. To achieve all of this would not be impossible, but very expensive, and therefore highly improbable. We lack the political will to pay the price for a truly pro-life society.

The above paragraph certainly does not sound optimistic, but I am not suggesting that we sink into pessimism and fatalism. A better attitude goes by the name "meliorism" from the Latin word *melior* meaning "better." William James and John Dewey used this term to express the notion that while the optimist thinks the world is so nice that no change is necessary, and the pessimist thinks the world is so flawed that no change is possible, the meliorist believes in and works for ways to make things better. The task of ethical thinking consists of striving to attain the best possible understanding of reality, its good aspects as well as its bad ones, and working to make improvements. So, we need to examine our individual and collective attitude toward pregnant women and unborn babies who stand outside the web of family, social, and economic security. What acts can we perform and what connections can we help to build that will assure that the mothers and children can take their places in a well-integrated society and achieve their human potential?

Just as we need to improve our reverence for our relations with the unborn, we have a lot of room for improvement with those who are near death and dying. We may easily forget that we ourselves were once unborn, but only with a super effort of denial can we forget that most of us will some day be among the dying. We can be exempted from the class of dying people only if our death comes very suddenly. Besides ourselves, nearly all of us face the dying of those whom we love and feel deeply connected to. Our loyalty belongs not only to the web of human life, as in the case of the unborn, but also to whatever relations we had with the dying, especially family and friends. But what of those who die alone with no family and friends. They were once connected to us by a common geography, or by citizenship, or at least as fellow human beings. We and they did not tend these relationships very well. Yet, when we hear of a person dying alone, we ought to remember the words of poet John Donne, "Send not to know for whom the bell toll; it tolls for thee." If Donne has it right, we are all connected; what we lack is awareness.

For those dying persons to whom we have the duty that comes with conscious relationships we can connect to them ethically, neither denying their death by needlessly prolonging it, nor by hustling them along. Reverence for relations requires us to act supportively toward the terminally ill as they pass through the stages of natural dying with as much love and comfort as possible. And while most of us have neither the resources nor the ability to be there for those who die alone, we can provide support for those who can help them.

Social Justice and Criminal Justice

The notion of social justice has acquired a bad name among some political conservatives who think that it can only mean egalitarian distribution of wealth and that it signifies a code-word for *socialism*. As I argued in Chapter Seven, social justice signifies a structure in which each person has the opportunity to develop his or her potential. Any structure that would limit a person because of race, ethnicity, gender, religion, or any other arbitrary characteristic, would be unjust. Further, failing to provide opportunity to children who are born into situations that do not afford them a chance to grow and develop would likewise be unjust. What do we do about those who are poor but have no evident potential for growth because they lack the skills and the ability to learn the skills necessary for employment in our complex world? Finding work for everyone and training them to perform some kind of work costs more than simply supporting the poor. Sadly, we fall into such a state of disintegration, that we remain unwilling to pay the price of finding a place for everyone.

A person who commits a crime of any sort damages the relationships that healthy people and healthy communities require. A person who commits an act of fraud in business weakens or destroys the trust and confidence that enable the business community to thrive. An act of violence against persons or property destroys personal confidence and greatly impedes the ability of the victim to maintain relationships with other people. Punishment of criminals expresses the intention of society to stand with the victim and share outrage at the wrong that was done. The criminals remain members of the community, and although society rightly imposes a punishment on them, we collectively should do whatever we can to enable the criminals to get their lives back together and take a place in society.

The crime of murder is a case apart in terms of the evil done. The life of the victim is irrevocably lost and the relationships that he or she once enjoyed are shattered beyond repair. Nothing can undo the harm that the murder has inflicted. The degree of harm gives some credence to those who argue that only by the death penalty can we express the enormity of our outrage at the crime. And yet, by refusing to deliberately kill a person who is in custody, we express an even stronger respect for the biological bond of life on which all the other relationships rest. Loyalty to human life itself can serve as the rock bottom of every relationship between persons to each other and to the society that we share.

Personal and Social Integrity

The first chapter of this book distinguished desirable actions from those that we merely desire. Desires motivate us to act, but we often desire things that are harmful to ourselves, and others, or things that simply waste our time, passively preventing us from fulfilling our potential as human beings. We can rate a goal desirable when all of the foreseen consequences of achieving the goal are worth the cost in effort, time, and treasure. For individuals, worthwhile goals enable them to actualize their potential by integrating their feelings, thoughts, words, and actions as persons dedicated to their causes. Such persons exhibit the quality that we admire as integrity. In their dealing with other individuals and with social relationships they do their part in bringing about integration, which allows each individual the most freedom to develop his or her unique potential while working together for the common cause of a just and prosperous society.

Striving to nourish the good, which Royce calls "teleological harmony," provides a standard for deciding which actions are right and which are wrong. Often the issue involves not right and wrong but rather choosing the better path, or the least of the evils that might confront us. Moral imagination can sometimes free us from false dilemmas and find good options that were not readily observable. Our full moral development as human beings depend on the ability to find and loyally follow a life that leads to personal and social integration.

ENDNOTES

Chapter 1. Leading Principles of Ethics

[1] Peirce's letter is attached to Frank Oppenheim's *Royce's Mature Ethics* (Notre Dame, Indiana: University of Notre Dame Press, 1993) Appendix C, 241-242. Further discussion is found in John Clendenning, *The Life and Thought of Josiah Royce* (Nashville: Vanderbilt University Press, 1999) 358-359. Peirce wrote the letter discussing uberty in response to receiving Royce's *Problem of Christianity*. He hoped to do a thorough study of the work when his health improved. His health did not improve and he died ten months later. Clendenning describes Royce's approval of Peirce's letter and agrees with Frank Oppenheim that Royce's emphasis on the "fecundity of aggregation" parallels Peirce's uberty.

[2] These leading ideas are found throughout Royce's work. A good summary of these ideas is expressed in the last year of his life. At the end of his mid-term exam for an ethics course, in February, 1916, he instructed his students as part of a case study involving a mother and daughter: "In particular, show what bearing each of the 'three leading ethical ideas' has on this case; that is, show how: (1) the idea of independence; (2) the idea of the Good; and (3) the idea of Duty stand related to the ethical needs of these two women. Oppenheim *Ethics,* Appendix B, 240.

[3] The role of loyalty and how it addresses the paradox of autonomy and duty will be explained in the section below on "loyalty as the cardinal virtue."

[4] Josiah Royce, *Studies of Good and Evil: A Series of Essays upon the Problems of Philosophy and Life* (Hamden, CT: Archon Books, 1964), 14.

[5] Charles Peirce makes a distinction between an opinion and a belief. Like all pragmatists, Peirce holds that we believe something only if we are prepared to act on it. Opinions include things that we may hold tentatively as true, such as scientific hypotheses, but which involve no practical commitment on our part. For the sake of the current discussion on Royce, the distinction does not make a difference, and the terms "opinions" and "beliefs" may be used interchangeably as statements that we hold as true.

[6] Robert Solomon, *Ethics and Excellence* (*New* York: Oxford University Press, 1992), 3.

[7] John Dewey, *Reconstruction in Philosophy* (Mineola, New York: Dover Publications, 2004), 94.

[8] Bruce Kuklick, *A History of Philosophy in America,* 1720 -2000 (Oxford: Clarendon Press, 2001), 236. The philosophical movement known as Logical Positivism, also called Logical Empiricism, maintained that the only meaningful statements are those that refer to observable facts. Ethical statements are merely emotive; they express the feelings of the speaker. Kuklick describes the powerful influence that logical Positivism had on American Philosophy in the middle of the twentieth century, 257 and the enduring influence that it has on our culture. "Long after even the most committed scientific philosophers rejected logical empiricism this philosophy gained a new lease on life when defended by scholars in other disciplines." 268.

[9] John Dewey, *The Quest for Certainty* (New York: YTTLP and Ives Company, Internet Archives, Universal Library), 260.

[10] This statement has been attributed to several different writers including Ralph Waldo Emerson and Samuel Smiles. According to *Bartlett's,* it is anonymous. *Quoteland* .com. January 2, 2009.

[11] Tom Morris, *If Aristotle Ran General Motors: The New Soul of Business* (New York: Henry Holt and Company, 1997), 94.

Chapter 2. The Neglected Concept of Loyalty

[12] The works referred to and which will be the main sources for this work include; *Studies in Good and Evil* (1898), *The World and the Individual* (1899 -1901) *The Philosophy of Loyalty* (1907), *The Sources of Religious Insight* (1912), *and The Problem of Christianity* (1913).

[13] SGE 18.

[14] Ibid.

[15] Jacquelyn Ann K. Kegley, *Josiah Royce in Focus:* (Bloomington: Indiana University Press, 2008.) Kegley explains Royce's role as a psychologist in chapter two, "The Self."

[16] Josiah Royce, *The Philosophy of Loyalty* (Nashville: University of Vanderbilt Press, 1995), 9. Royce calls this definition "preliminary." Later in *Philosophy of Loyalty* he offers a definition of loyalty that he considers more complete metaphysically: *"Loyalty is the will to believe in something eternal and to express that belief in the practical life of a human being"* Italics in original, 166. Following Royce's example of postponing the full definition until the latter part of *The Philosophy of Loyalty*, this book will proceed with the preliminary definition. Chapter 10 will show how the complete definition is incorporated in the content of Chapters 3 – 9.

[17] PL 51.

[18] PL 58.

[19] Tom Morris, *If Aristotle Ran General Motors,* 126.

[20] PL 63.

[21] This phrase, which is used throughout this book, is suggested by Frank Oppenheim's book by that title. *Reverence for the Relations of Life* (University of Notre Dame Press, 2005).

Chapter 3. The Self as an Ethical Task

[22] Aristotle, *Nicomachean Ethics* in *Basic Works of Aristotle,* edited by Richard M. McKeon (New York: Random House Books, 1966), 935.

[23] In *The Soul of Classical American Philosophy* (Albany: State University of New York Press, 2007), 97. I explain harmony as the goal of every idea, life plan, and loyal act in the context of Royce's description of the task of the philosopher in response to letter from Peirce on uberty as cited in Chapter 1. Here I will present these three aspects of Royce's teleology in the context of our ethical duty to actualize our selves.

[24] Josiah Royce, *The World and the Individual,* First Series (Gloucester, MA: Peter Smith,1976), 22.

[25] *The World and the Individual,* Second series, 275-276.

[26] *Philosophy of Loyalty,* 43.

[27] William James, *The Principles of Psychology Vol. 1* (New York: Dover Publications, 1950) 488.

[28] Josiah Royce, *The Sources of Religious Insight* (New York: Charles Scribners Sons,

1912), 87.

[29] Scott Peck, *The Road Less Traveled: A New Psychology of Love, Traditional Values and Spiritual Growth* (New York: Simon and Schuster, 1978), 273.

[30] Charles Sanders Peirce, *Collected Papers,* CP 1.615 (Cambridge: Harvard University Press) Electronic Version, InteLex Corporation.

[31] Josiah Royce, *The Problem of Christianity* (Washington, D. C. The Catholic University of America Press, 2001), 281-291.

[32] *The Problem of Christianity,* 307.

[33] *The Problem of Christianity,* 307.

[34] *The Problem of Christianity,* 308.

[35] *The Problem of Christianity*, 3-4.

[36] *The Philosophy of Loyalty*, 67.

[37] *The Sources of Religious Insight*, 232 -241.

[38] Jacquelyn Ann Kegley, *Josiah Royce in Focus* (Bloomington: Indian University Press 2008) 204 -206.

Chapter 4. Friendship, Love, and Personal Development

[39] SRI 44

[40] PL 12

[41] Josiah Royce, *The World and the Individual*, Second Series, 276. Royce works out the relationship between the individual and society in his Two Series of Gifford Lectures of 1899 and 1900, especially Lecture VI of the Second Series, "The Human Self."

[42] Scott Peck, *The Road Less Traveled: A New Psychology of Love, Traditional Values and Spiritual Growth* (New York: Simon and Schuster, 1978), 1. The opening sentence of Peck's book is "Life is difficult." He contends that most people make it even more difficult by imagining that life should be easy. Life is about spiritual growth, but since many people try to avoid facing the difficulty of growth, the road is "less traveled."

[43] Lawrence Kohlberg, *The Philosophy of Moral Development* (San Francisco: Harper and Row, 1981.) Kohlberg's Six Stages of Moral Development are well known and often quoted. The description here would fit his Stage 3, Interpersonal Concordance, which would most typically be found in an early teenage or pre-teenage child. According to Kohlberg, a person's moral development may stop at any stage.

[44] Aristotle, *Nicomachean Ethics, Book VIII*, 2 -4, in *The Basic Works of Aristotle*, 105 -1063.

[45] Aristotle, *Nicomachaen Ethics, Book VIII, 1* in *The Basic Works of Aristotle,* 1058.

[46] Readers familiar with the history of Utilitarianism may notice a similarity of this idea with that of Jeremy Bentham's "Felicific Calculus." Economist Robert Heilbroner summed up Bentham's take on the idea that we live to maximize pleasure calling it, "...a philosophical view of humanity as so many profit-and-loss calculators, each busily arranging his life to maximize the pleasure of his psychic adding machine." Robert Heilbroner, *The Worldly Philosophers* (New York: Simon and Schuster, 1961), 146.

[47] Mihaly Csikszentmihalyi, *Flow: The Psychology of Optimal Experience* (New York: Harper and Row, 1990), 46-47. Csikszentmihalyi distinguishes between pleasure and enjoyment. Pleasure is passive and requires no effort. Enjoyment involves investing psychic energy in challenging activities and may or may not be pleasurable.

[48] St. Thomas Aquinas. *Summa Theologica.* Question 6, Article 1, and Question 48, article 3.

[49] *The Spirit of Modern Philosophy,* 406.

[50] *The Spirit of Modern Philosophy,* 430. As stated above in note 9, while Royce held the notion of a universal mind, he also affirms the uniqueness of the individual. The self achieves its meaning as a unique individual by its particular and irreplaceable ethical role in the universal order. In Royce's words: *"By this meaning of my life-plan, by this possession of an ideal, by this Intent always to remain another than my fellow despite my divinely planned unity with them—-by this and not by possession of any Soul Substance, I am defined and created a self."* Emphasis in the original. Josiah Royce, *The World and the Individual, Second Series,* (Gloucester, MA: Peter Smith, 1976) 276.

[51] Plato's "Symposium" in *Plato: The Collected Dialogues* edited by Edith Hamilton and Huntington Cairns (Princeton, NJ: Princeton University Press, Bollingen Series, 1961), 542 -546.

[52] Rollo May: *Love and Will* (New York: Dell Publishing Company, 1969), 73. May presented a thoughtful discussion of erotic love in the 60's at a time when it seemed to be a casualty in the sexual revolution.

[53] Royce, to the best of my knowledge, did not write about erotic love or about beauty. Royce explains in a letter to his friend, Richard Cabot, that he loves beauty, especially in nature, music, and poetry, but did not feel qualified to write about it. John Clendenning editor, *The Letters of Josiah Royce* (Chicago: The University of Chicago Press, 1970, 577-578.

[54] Scott Peck, *The Road Less Traveled*, 84-93.

[55] Carl Jung, "Development of Personality," in *Collected Works, 17* (New York: Pantheon Books, 1953 -1979), 198.

[56] Scott Peck, *The Road Less Traveled*, 81.

[57] Erich Fromm, *The Art of Loving* (New York: Harper and Row, 1956), 22.

[58] This section is based loosely on the structure found in Erich Fromm's *The Art of Loving.*

[59] William James's, *The Varieties of Religious Experience* (New York: The New American Library, 1958), 383.

[60] Josiah Royce, *The Spirit of Modern Philosophy* Boston Houghton Miflin,1892 (NABU Reprint) 441.

[61] *Ibid*

[62] Ibid, 446.

[63] Ibid 467

[64] Royce maintained that the Christian doctrine of life holds value even for non-Christians since it expresses in symbolic terms the universal principle of life. The *Logos,* usually translated as Word," refers to the creative principle that brings order and harmony into reality. In the first chapter of the Gospel of John, the Logos is identified as Christ. "And the Word was made flesh and dwelt among us."

[65] Josiah Royce, *Sources of Religious Insight* (New York: Charles Scribners Sons, 1912), 75.

[66] Frank Oppenheim, *Reverence for the Relations of Life* (Notre Dame, IN: University of Notre Dame Press, 2005), 2.

[67] Thomas A. Mappes, "Sexual Morality and the Concept of Using Another Person," in *Social Ethics: Morality and Social Policy,* Sixth Edition (New York: Mc Graw-Hill, Higher Education, 2002), 170 -183.

[68] At the time of this writing gay marriage is controversial political issue in the United States, recognized in some states but not others. The fact that advocates on both sides express such strong feeling shows that *marriage* still stands out as a very significant aspect of life in the twenty first century.

[69] Of course there are individuals, most often women, who do a good job of raising children alone. This situation may be caused by death, military service, divorce, or abandonment, and is usually unfortunate if not tragic. I assume that most such parents would prefer to share the child-raising with a person who loves them and the children and shows loyalty to their relationship.

[70] Ella Lyman Cabot, *Our Part in the World* (Boston: The Beacon Press, 1918, published by Forgotten books, 2012), 125.

[71] Cabot ,126.

Chapter 5. Business Ethics

[72] Robert Solomon, *Ethics and Excellence: Cooperation and Integrity in Business* (New York: Oxford University Press, 1993), 3-5.

[73] Michael Lewis, *Boomerang: Travels in the Third New World* (New York: W. W. Norton & Company, 2011) xi.

[74] Lewis, 15. Lewis shows how, at the time of his writing, the financial crisis was playing out, not only in Iceland, but also, in different ways according to each nation's character, in Greece, Ireland, Germany, and the United States.

[75] John Steele Gordon, *An Empire of Wealth: The Epic History of American Economic Power* (New York: Harper Collins Publishers, 2004), 211.

[76] A reader might question the judgment of the water treatment manager, and after gathering all of the information, may argue whether he made the right decision. But the manager had to choose quickly between two bad outcomes, and did not have time to argue. I was not able to do a follow-up, but the company was reputable and I assume that they put a contingency plan in place in case this situation happened again and also took precautions to avert it from ever happening again.

[77] *Fortune,* (July 10, 2006).

[78] I don't know if there was really more greed in the 1980s than in other decades. But a survey of the term "decade of greed" shows that the media gave that name to the decade of the 1980s. It was a time when students could say without embarrassment that their main goal if life was to make a lot of money.

[79] Robert Solomon, 35-36.

[80] Trotter, Griffith 197. quoting from Royce's *Philosophy of Loyalty*.

[81] Trotter, 196 -201.

[82] Jacquelyn Ann K. Kegley, *Josiah Royce in Focus* (Bloomington: Indiana University Press, 2008) 61. Kegley traces the idea of the development of the moral person through Royce's works from 1880 to 1913.

[83] Trevino, Linda K and Katherine A. Nelson, *Managing Business Ethics: Straight Talk About How To Do It Right* (Hoboken, NJ: John Wiley and Sons, Inc., 2007), 180 -181.

[84] Trevino and Nelson, 183.

[85] Chris Lowney. *Heroic Leadership: Best Practices From a 450 Year-Old Company that Changed the World* (Chicago: Loyola Press, 2003), 179.

[86] Frank M. Oppenheim, S. J., *Reverence for the Relations of Life*, 1. Oppenheim cites the philosopher Josiah Royce, who in his history of California noted that the difference between communities that took root and thrived, and those that experienced "boom and bust," was that the members of the former showed "reverence for the relations of life."

Chapter 6. Living Ethically in a Consumerist Society

[87] Frank Oppenheim, *Reverence for the Relations of Life*, 2.

[88] *Ibid.*

[89] Rudolph Otto, *The Idea of the Holy* (Oxford: Oxford University Press, 1958), 31.

[90] The philosophy of "Positivism" should not be confused with other movements such as "Positive thinking" and positive psychology. Positivism as used in the text refers to the philosophical belief that no statements about reality have meaning except those that can be empirically verified by the "positive sciences."

[91] Bruce Kuklick, *A History of Philosophy in America* (New York: Oxford University Press, 2001). Kuklick observes that logical

positivism, also called logical empiricism, lost much of its earlier influence in philosophy beginning in the 1960s, and philosophy in general became isolated and ignored. But the influence of logical empiricism endured in disciplines such as political science, sociology and economics. As Kuklick describes the attitude in American universities at the end of the 20th century; "Long after even the most committed scientific philosophers rejected logical empiricism, this philosophy gained a new lease of life when defended by scholars in other disciplines." 268.

[92] J. Donald Hughes, "The Ancient Roots of Our Ecological Crisis" in *Environmental Ethics: Divergence and Convergence,* Second Edition, edited by Susan J. Armstrong and Richard G. Botzler (New York: McGraw Hill, 1998.)

[93] Rene Descartes, *Discourse on the Method of Rightly Conducting the Reason and Seeking for Truth in the Sciences,* in *The Philosophical Works of Descartes, Volume I* translated by Elizabeth Haldane and G. R. T. Ross (Cambridge: University Press, 1968), 119.

[94] For this expression I am indebted to William James, who addressing this very problem in his 1881 lecture, "Reflex Action and Theism", asserted: "At a single stroke, (religious faith) changes the dead blank *it* of the world into a living *thou,* with whom the whole man may have dealings." William James, *The Will to Believe and Other Essays* (New York: Dover Publications, 1956), 127.

[95] Matthew Fox, "The Soul of Nature," in Armstrong and Botzler, 231.

[96] Karl Marx, "Private Property and Communism" in *The Economic and Philosophic Manuscripts of 1844* (New York: International Publishers, 1964), 139.

[97] It is not my intention here to present the history of Romanticism or to trace the love of nature before that time. My

purpose is to point out that Environmental Ethics developed for the most part in the second half of the twentieth century and that it is compatible with Roycean thought.

[98] Aldo Leopold , "The Land Ethic" in *Environmental Ethics: What Really Matters, What Really Works,* edited by David Schmidtz and Elizabeth Willott (New York: Oxford University Press, 2002), 28.

[99] Ann Chisholm *Philosophers of the Earth: Conversations with Ecologists* (New York: E. P. Dutton and Company) 1972), 63, quoting Aldo Leopold's *Sand County Almanac.*

[100] William Baxter, "People or Penguins" in *Doing Ethics: Moral Reasoning and Contemporary Issues Second Edition, edited by Lewis Vaughn* (New York: W. W. Norton and Company, 2010), 480.

[101] The decision makers include the executives of the coal companies as well as the politicians who protect the mining interests from the EPA. The fact that politicians with little concern for the environment win elections in states such as West Virginia and Kentucky indicates that the majority of the people in these states comply with these decisions.

[102] Ellen F. Davis, *Scripture, Culture, and Agriculture: An Agrarian Reading of the Bible* (New York: Cambridge University Press, 2009), 13. As a theologian Davis takes on the task of showing how the Bible can lead us to a more ethical treatment of the land. But she explicitly stands on common ground with secular environmentalists and agrarians who share her respect for the land.

[103] Josiah Royce, The *Spirit of Modern Philosophy, 446.*

[104] ST 1, 48 ad. 2, cited in Larry Rasmussen, *Earth Community/ Earth Ethics* (New York: Orbis Books, Maryknoll, 1996), 193.

[105] E. F. Schumacher, *A Guide for the Perplexed* (New York: Harper and Row, 1977), 134.

[106] Wendell Berry, "*The Gift of Good Land* (New York: North Point Press, Farrar, Straus,
and Giroux, 1982), 178.

[107] Wendell Berry, *The Gift of Good Land,* 274-275. Theologian, Ellen Davis author of *Scripture, Culture, and Agriculture: An Agrarian Reading of the Bible,* with an introduction by Wendell Berry, is developing theological insights compatible with Berry's work.

[108] Dave Foreman. "Putting Earth First" in Armstrong and Botzler, 449.

[109] James Nash. *Loving Nature: Ecological Integrity and Christian Responsibility* (Nashville: Abingdon, 1991), 181.

[110] Holmes Rolston III, "Environmental Ethics; Values and Duties in a Natural World," Armstrong and Botzler, 75.

Chapter 7. Social and Economic Justice

[111] Alan Gewirth. "Economic Justice: Concepts and Criteria" in *Economic Justice: Private Rights and Public Responsibilities,* edited by Kenneth Kipnis and Diana T. Meyers (Totowa, New Jersey: Roman and Allanheld, 1985), 8.

[112] *Wheeling Intelligencer,* April 8, 2009.

[113] Irving Kristol, "A Capitalist Conception of Justice," in W. Michael Hoffman and Robert Frederick, *Business Ethics: Readings and Cases in Corporate Morality,* Third Edition (New York: McGraw-Hill, 1995), 72.

At the time of this writing, some politicians, notably Senator and presidential candidate Bernie Sanders of Vermont, identify themselves as a Democratic Socialists. In fact they are not Socialist according to the traditional meaning of the term as expressed in this chapter.

[115] The 19th century ideas of Marx can be examined apart from the dictatorships that emerged in the 20th century under Marx' banner. The question of whether Marxian ideas inevitably lead to oppressive dictatorship stands as a relevant question, but one that cannot be taken up here. Marx believed that the liberation of the workers, and in fact all human beings, required the abolition of private property, which would come about through revolution. There are many forms of socialism that are reformist and moderate.

[116] Karl Marx. *The German Ideology* (New York: International Publishers, 1970), 53.

[117] Robert Nozick, "Distributive Justice," excerpted from *Anarchy, State, and Utopia,* in Hoffman and Frederick, 58.

[118] Friedrich A. Hayek, *The Road to Serfdom* (University of Chicago Press, 1944), 79.

[119] John Rawls. *A Theory of Justice* (Cambridge, Massachusetts: The Belknap Press of Harvard University Press, 1971), 151.

[120] Irving Kristol, "A Capitalist Conception of Justice," in Hoffman and Frederick, 69.

[121] Thomas Hobbes argued that to end the state of war of all against each, we give our rights over to a sovereign. Sovereigns may dictate the terms of property ownership. For Hobbes, property ownership, like everything else is a matter of might, not right.

[122] Michael Novak. *The Catholic Ethic and the Spirit of Capitalism* (New York: The Free Press, 1993), 62-88.

[123] Sandra B. Rosenthal and Rogene A. Buchholz, *Rethinking Business Ethics: A Pragmatic Approach* (New York: Oxford University Press, 2000), 7 -18.

[124] Rosenthal and Buchholz, 8.

Chapter 8. Ethical Issues Involving the Beginning of Life

[125] The incident described here happened in the early 1980s. A January, 2007 article in the*New York Times*, describing the new Democratic majority's attempt to move toward a moderate position defined "common ground" as their mantra.

126 At the time of this writing, the Supreme Court seems to have shifted in a way favorable to the

"pro-life" side but has not yet expressed an opinion on this issue.

[127] My purpose in this section is to show some of the more influential and diverse positions on abortion and cannot include the wealth of scholarship on this issue. One example not included here is the utilitarian view as developed by L. W. Sumner. His position as stated in "A Moderate View" (PubMed Adv. Bioethic.1997, 2, 203-221) holds that a human has an interest to defend only when it can feel sensation. So from Sumner's point of view the position by Noonan, given below is too narrow because it would defend human life before it is sensitive. He also opposes the position of Mary Ann Warren because it fails to defend the life of a late term fetus or even an infant or small child who has not yet attained full personhood.

[128] John T. Noonan, *Morality of Abortion,* "An Almost Absolute Value in History," in *Morality of Abortion: Legal and Historical Perspectives,* edited by Noonan (Cambridge MA: Harvard University Press, 1970), 51.

[129] Mary Ann Warren, "On the Moral and Legal Status of Abortion" in *Social Ethics* Sixth Edition, edited by Thomas Mappes and Jane S. Zembaty, 14-21.

[130] Don Marquis, "Why Abortion is Immoral," *Journal of Philosophy* Vol. 86, No 4, April, 1989, 183-202. Marquis explicitly omits issues that he acknowledges as important for a complete ethic of abortion including whether abortion is permissible "before implementation, abortion when the life of a woman is threatened by pregnancy, or abortion after rape." Paragraph 3. His intention is to

"show that abortion is, except possibly in rare cases, seriously immoral..." Paragraph 1.

[131] Don Marquis, Paragraph 23.

[132] Justice Harry A. Blackmun, *Majority Opinion in Roe v. Wade,* in Mappes and Zembaty, 39-44.

[133] She has since revealed her identity and proclaimed herself a pro-life, born-again Christian.

Chapter 9. Ethical Issues Involving the End of Life

[134] Statement of the House of Delegates of the AMA, December 4, 1973, quoted by James Rachels in "Active and Passive Euthanasia" in Mappes and Zembaty, 68.

[135] James Rachels, "Active and Passive Euthanasia" in Mappes and Zembaty, 68 – 72.

[136] Daniel Callahan provides a strong defense of the traditional position and the distinction between killing and allowing to die in "When Self-Determination Runs Amok, *Hastings Center Report,* March-April, 1992.

[137] Tom Morris, *If Aristotle Ran General Motors: The New Soul of Business,* 94.

[138] Mwalimu Imara, "Dying as the Last Stage of Growth" in Elizabeth Kubler-Ross, *Death the Final Stage of Growth* (New York: Touchstone Books, 1975), 150. Also, Scott Peck, *Denial of the Soul* (New York: Harmony Books, 1997), 203-204.

[139] Scott Peck, *Denial of the Soul,* 55.

Chapter 10. Punishment and Capital Punishment

[140] Immanuel Kant. *Foundations of the Metaphysics of Morals* (New York: The Liberal Arts Press, 1959).

[141] "To Execute or Not: A Question of Cost," MSNBC.com – Associated Press, updated March 3, 2009.

[142] Ernest Van den Haag, "The Ultimate Punishment: A Defense, in Lewis Vaughn, *Doing Ethics: Moral Reasoning and Contemporary Issues* (New York: W. W. Norton, 2008), 161.

[143] Furman v. Georgia 1972. U. S. Supreme Court 408 U. S. 238 (1972).

Chapter 11: Loyalty and Reverence for Relationship as a Universal Ethical Standard

[144] Josiah Royce, *The Philosophy of Loyalty*, 9.

[145] Al Gini describes this phenomenon using the terms ethnocentrism and Konrad Lorenz's term "pseudo-speciation." Al Gini, *Why It's Hard to Be Good* (New York: Routledge, 2008), 42-45.

[146] Josiah Royce, *The Philosophy of Loyalty*, 51-69.

[147] *The Philosophy of Loyalty*, 166.

[148] Josiah Royce, "Loyalty and Insight," in *William James and Other Essays on the Philosophy of Life* (New York: The MacMillan Company, 1912) 77 -78.

[149] Josiah Royce, *The Sources of Religious Insight*, 171.

[150] *Ibid.*, 206.

[151] *Ibid.*, 206.

[152] *Ibid.*, 205.

[153] "Loyalty and Insight," 73 -75.

[154] Abraham Maslow, *Toward a Psychology of Being*, Second Edition (New York: Van Norstrand, 1968), 81-82.

[155] Tom Morris, *If Aristotle Ran General Motor*, 118. Morris makes no reference to Royce, but his excellent book on business ethics also provides a general ethics perfectly compatible with Royce.

[156] It may be that a person has to go through a period of disorganization which breaks down unworkable patterns of thought and behavior, before they can come into greater harmony and integration. See *Transformational Stories; Voices for True Healing in Mental Health*, Susko, M. (ed.) 2019.

[157] Josiah Royce, *The Sources of Religious Insight*, 87.

[158] Frank Oppenheim, *Royce's Mature Philosophy of Religion* (Notre Dame, Indiana: University of Notre Dame Press, 1987), 102. Oppenheim refers to Royce's *Source of Religious Insight*, page 207, where Royce says of loyalty, that it "...shows you the gracious and eternal miracle of a spiritual realm, where whatever fortunes and miracles and divine beings there may be, you, in so far as you are loyal, are and are to be always at home."

Did you love *Ethics and the Full-Breasted Richness of Life*? Then you should read *The Neglected Doctrine of the Holy Spirit: Josiah Royce as a Guide to Renewing Theology*[1] by Richard Mullin!

The Holy Spirit is a dimension of Godhood which is not given much attention, yet one that is critical for our spiritual development. In this work Richard Mullin shows how the contribution of American Philosophers at the turn of the 20th century can serve as a basis to reenvision theology. Importantly, he distinguishes the historical church with all its shortcomings and the Universal or "Beloved Community." Read this work if you are seeking a mature spiritual vision and one for which the church is a task that remains to be completed.

Read more at https://www.letphilosophyshine.com/.

---

1. https://books2read.com/u/3k51zO

2. https://books2read.com/u/3k51zO

About the Author

Richard P. Mullin earned his PhD, in philosophy and taught philosophy at Wheeling Jesuit University for thirty years. He also taught Business Ethics in the MBA program. He has lectured in American philosophy in Slovenia and Slovakia and frequently read papers at the meetings of the Society for the Advancement of American Philosophy. In *The Soul of Classical American Philosophy: The Ethical and Spiritual Insights of William James, Josiah Royce, and Charles Sanders Pierce (SUNY Press2007)*, he portrays the governing ideas of the founders of American Pragmatism.

Read more at https://www.letphilosophyshine.com/.

www.ingramcontent.com/pod-product-compliance
Lightning Source LLC
Chambersburg PA
CBHW032305070726

47590CB00015B/751